Waterfowling on the Chesapeake, 1819–1936

WATERFOWLING

on the CHESAPEAKE
1819-1936

C. John Sullivan

THE JOHNS HOPKINS UNIVERSITY PRESS   BALTIMORE & LONDON

© 2003 The Johns Hopkins University Press
All rights reserved. Published 2003
Manufactured in China
on acid-free paper

9 8 7 6 5 4 3 2 1

The Johns Hopkins University Press
2715 North Charles Street
Baltimore, Maryland 21218-4363
www.press.jhu.edu

Library of Congress Cataloging-in-Publication Data
Sullivan, C. John.
  Waterfowling on the Chesapeake, 1819–1936 /
C. John Sullivan.
    p.   cm.
Includes index.
  ISBN 0-8018-7155-7 (hardcover : alk. paper)
  1. Waterfowl shooting—Chesapeake Bay Region
(Md. and Va.)—History. 2. Chesapeake Bay Region
(Md. and Va.)—History. I. Title.
SK331 .S85 2002
799.2'44'0916347—dc21   2002005382

A catalog record for this book is available from the
British Library.

I affectionately dedicate this book to my grandson,

BENJAMIN BLAIR SULLIVAN,

in hopes that he will someday cherish

this part of our history

as much as I.

✦ CONTENTS ✦

❋ ACKNOWLEDGMENTS ❋

As the final manuscript for this book was being prepared, I started to wonder about acknowledgments. Whom would I thank? How many had helped see this book to its end? Who had helped me along the way? My search for history and all those things that make it come alive for me is never-ending; this is what drives me. My grandparents started me on this search. I owe a debt to my grandfathers, who shared with me their days on the railroad and working at the mill; to uncles, who told me of the war and showed me how to drive a team of horses; to my parents, who showed me where my family came from and what my county used to look like. My loving wife put up with my search, and my dear son has traveled by my side to auctions, to attics, to decoy carvers' shops. To them I owe an enormous debt of gratitude, a debt that I will never be able to repay.

At the Johns Hopkins University Press, I thank Robert J. Brugger, who entrusted this work to me and who became a friend along the way. His assistant, Melody Herr, provided advice and encouragement; and I thank Jack Holmes, Director of Development, who brought a smile to my face at times of frustration. Copyeditor Anne M. Whitmore ironed the kinks out of my work.

I thank Barbara Wells Sarudy, former director of the Maryland Humanities Council, never further away than a phone call, who allowed me to vent and who advised me on a myriad of topics.

I am incredibly blessed to have a few old friends who support me day to day, and without these people this book might not have come to fruition. I thank Mary Elizabeth Miklochik, my professional colleague and an accomplished artist, who provided assistance on the chapters about the Crisfield carvers and teal and who encouraged me throughout the project. Next I need to thank Margaret Anne Reel, my close friend since high school, who went out of her way to lend her editorial expertise and skilled facility with language to help me synthesize my thoughts and incorporate quoted material into the text. And finally I want to thank Kaye Brooks Bushel, whom I first met when she was an assistant attorney general. Her legal expertise over the years has been a tremendous help, and she researched the legislative time line for this book. She also served as a researcher, editor, and indexer for the entire project; but most importantly, Kaye is an empathetic confidant and advisor.

Special thanks to friends Bruce Carlin, Robert N. Hockaday, Jr., and Patrick S. O'Neill, who have always been there for me.

I owe thanks to the late John Pusey and his son, Joel Pusey, who have been friends, storytellers, and suppliers of some wonderful things for many years. I also deeply appreciate the friendship of the late Mary Helen Cadwalader and her brother, Benjamin Cadwalader, who were kind and generous hosts and shared a wealth of knowledge with me regarding the Gunpowder Neck.

I am very grateful to some others whose generosity, friendship, and sharing helped me finish this book: Ken Callahan, Thomas R. Chambers, Roger J. Colburn, Anthony Hillman, Edward Schmidbauer, Henry H. Stansbury, Vance C. Strausburg, J. Fife Symington, Jr., Donald Walker, Zack Ward, Harry C. Weiskittel III, Grayson C. Winterbottom III, Joe Engers of *Decoy* Magazine, Tom Nicholson of Media Dimensions, Chriss Smith of Taylor Made Photos, Mae M. Beck, Ronald H. McGrath, Nelson M. Berg, Homer N. Barnard, William W. Boyer, Sam Dyke, Darlene Mc-Call, the late James Holly Drennen, Jane Holly Corbin, Betty Drennen Langley, and my old friend Henry A. Fleckenstein, Jr.

Finally, I thank my dear mother and son, who hear my every thought, provide me with unflagging support, and never disappoint me. I do this for them.

I AM NOT SURE at what age I discovered the pair of old wooden decoys that rested on the hearth in my family's home. I do recall that I paid so much attention to them that my grandmother presented me with my very own decoy while I was still in grade school. It became the focal point of my bedroom in spite of the cowboy motif wallpaper.

That first decoy led to a lifelong avocation. By the age of eighteen, I was accumulating old wooden duck decoys with whatever money I could pull together. Then, in 1967, when I was a young man, R. Madison Mitchell, Jr., moved into an office next to mine. At that time, Mitchell's father was the most famous living decoy carver in the Upper Chesapeake region. He had learned his craft from an earlier generation of carvers in Havre de Grace, Maryland. Mitchell quickly recognized my passion for antique decoys and realized that I would pay more for the old ones that came into his father's decoy shop for new paint than I would for the new ones. My collection of historic decoys grew rapidly.

But merely having a large accumulation of old blocks of wood was not enough. I realized that I had grown to love the history of these wooden fowl and the stories they could tell. Hand-carved wooden decoys were an important part of the history of the Chesapeake region, and I needed to know who carved these early birds, how different styles had evolved and been passed down, how the decoys had been used and who had used them. My search for that history and the decoys and all the accoutrements of the duck hunter's rig has never stopped. It is a thirst that cannot be satisfied and that has led me into many attics.

It was January 10, 2001, when I rediscovered an important address; I had not seen it in my desk drawer for a number of years. My lifelong friend Henry A. Fleckenstein, Jr., had years before turned over to me Mrs. Frank Beck's name and address. He had met her when she walked into a decoy show in Essex, Maryland, in 1989. Henry had referred me to her, rather than pursuing the lead himself, because he thought the effort would be far greater than the reward. So there I went, looking for just one more great decoy—something that I've been seeking for more than thirty-five years now. I made the call and instantly knew that this would not be easy. The lady was ninety-four years old and lived in the same home that she and her husband had converted from a waterfront summer cottage to a year-round bungalow in 1940.

The appointment to visit her took considerable persuasion on my part. "I have nothing here, no more decoys, nothing from my husband's gunning days. But come to see me if you want, but there is nothing here, I'm telling you." So off I went, following directions to the neck district of Baltimore County. "I'm sorry—I told you there is nothing here, nothing, but here is how it was. He took out 'sports' from all around, they paid him good. See these duck prints here on the wall? These are Christmas cards that Walter Peacock sent, we had them framed, he was one of those 'sports.' Frank would take him out in his sinkbox. They liked to go out with Frank because he was so good with a gun, a five-time Maryland state trapshooting champion. But over the years the decoys and guns, they just sort of disappeared." So the visit went, looking at shooting trophies and souvenirs of a lifetime with the man she had loved, her paintings of the water and wildlife, and his trapshooting trophies, and gifts from wealthy sport gunners and trapshooting friends. After a warm and pleasant visit with a lovely lady, punctuated by her continuing apologies of having nothing left from the gunning days, I bid my farewell with one final request. "Can I just take one quick look in the garage?" "Well, go ahead," she responded, "but I'm telling you there is nothing out there."

I enter the garage—watering cans, a group of pink flamingoes—the old concrete ones resting next to their modern plastic cousins—rakes, bushel baskets, lawn mowers, lawn chairs, oil cans, gas cans, paint cans, storm windows, tire chains, and a pile of clear plastic sheeting. It's all here. I see something under the plastic. There they are—two or three plastic decoys. I move closer and lift up the plastic and a roll of rusty wire holding it in place. All of a sudden, I'm fifteen years old again, standing in Preston's Stationery Store on Main Street in Bel Air, in front of the plastic-wrapped adult magazines and the sign that says, "You must be 18 years old to look at these." My knees are shaking now and I feel weak. I'm having trouble lifting the plastic sheeting; my hands aren't working right. Then the plastic comes off a large wooden box that is full of ancient decoys. There's a good one, a bad one, one without a head, an awful head on a good old body, a good head on a really horrible body. I pick up each of them, savoring the smell, the dust and dirt of fifty years of rest. Here is a great branded one; here is a really early wing duck. Back to the house I go. "You found them, didn't you? I promised my son that no one else would get them. Would one of them make you happy? Then go ahead, but don't tell anyone, promise? And will you do one more thing? Promise me you'll come back." I certainly did.

Tales from the Days of Plenty

The Gunning Clubs

The Susquehanna Flats, the Gunpowder Neck, and the peninsulas formed by the other major rivers that flow into the Chesapeake Bay were the sight of fabulous gunning during the nineteenth century and the early decades of the twentieth century. This shoreline, extending from the mouth of the Susquehanna River to nearly the southern boundary of Virginia, with its numerous coves and guts, was ideal nesting and feeding grounds for abundant flocks of waterfowl.

Attracted by this abundance, wealthy sportsmen purchased or leased "gunning shores" along these waterways and formed exclusive clubs to engage in the sport of duck hunting. They generally named these clubs after the geographical location of the gunning shore, hence, the Spesutia Island Rod and Gun Club, the Taylor's Island Ducking and Fishing Club, the Marshy Point Ducking Club, the Carroll's Island Ducking Club, and the Seneca Ducking Club. The earliest known duck hunting club was formed in 1819 by a "society of gentlemen [from Baltimore] styling themselves The Maxwell's Point Gunning Club," according to the deed granting them title to 180 acres of land in Harford County, in the area of Sundricks (also called Swaderick) Creek and Maxwell's Point on the Gunpowder Neck, which is bounded by the Bush and Gunpowder Rivers as it extends out into the Bay. One of the members of that club was General Tobias E. Stansbury, who resided in Baltimore County on a 500-acre estate on Back River which included several good ducking points. Another gunning club, established as early as 1830, was on Carroll's Island, Baltimore County. The island is bounded by the Chesapeake Bay, the Seneca and Salt Petre Creeks, and the Gunpowder River.

The membership lists of these clubs were a virtual who's who of our nation's early financial markets and the captains of industry. They included sportsmen from New York, Philadelphia, and Baltimore. In 1880, the membership of the Carroll's Island Ducking Club included ten New Yorkers, ten Philadelphians, and only five Baltimoreans. The clubs built elaborate houses on their hunting shores to accommodate their gatherings and hunting parties. They maintained club journals and gunning logs and established precise hunting rules and guidelines for their members. These rules, although self-imposed, were strictly adhered to and represent the ef-

The clubhouse of the Taylor's Island Ducking and Fishing Club, situated on 400 acres of marshland at Locust Point on the Bush River

fort of some sportsmen to conserve an important natural resource. The surviving journals and logs provide a fascinating glimpse into the past.

The best gunning shores in Harford County were those on the Gunpowder and Bush River Necks. Their reputation was established very early. In 1802, Richard Colegate transferred 24 acres of land, described as "Colegates Fowling Ground Laying and being in Gunpowder Nick . . . and on the waters of Bush river," to a James Lytle. By the Civil War, the land belonged to the Cadwalader family, who owned over 7,000 acres out of the roughly 13,000 acres that comprised the Gunpowder Neck. Stretching at one point to more than ten miles in length, the Cadwalader land included nearly 40 miles of waterfront, down the eastern shore of the Gunpowder River to the point and up the western shore of the Bush River. General George Cadwalader of Philadelphia began buying land on the Gunpowder Neck in the 1840s; he eventually owned virtually the whole neck. His nephew, John Cadwalader of Philadelphia, inherited the property upon the general's death. The Cadwaladers built a large, timber hunting lodge on the high land of the smaller peninsula of Maxwell's Point, which projected into the Gunpowder River, and gunned with family and friends from that shore. Ducking boxes, the forerunner of ducking blinds for water use, were built into the peninsula. The property also contained stables and workout tracks for racehorses, greenhouses, and formal gardens. It was one of the greatest private preserves in the country.

The Cadwaladers leased gunning shores on the Gunpowder Neck to other sportsmen. In 1882, they leased the gunning rights to Tapler's Bar to John Cummings for $300 and those for Rickett's Point to R. T. Turner for

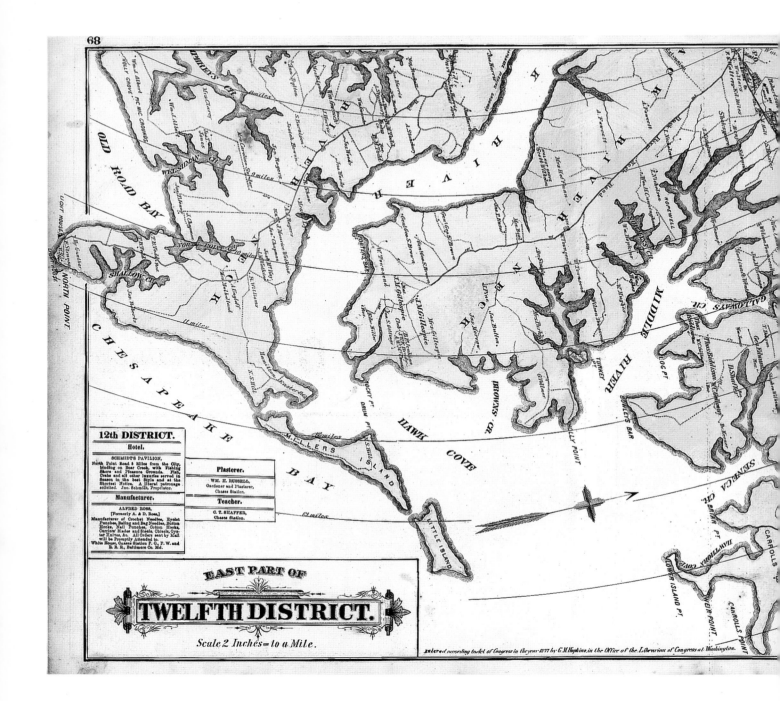

68

Entered according to act of Congress in the year 1877 by G.M. Hopkins, in the Office of the Librarian of Congress at Washington.

12th DISTRICT.

Hotel.

SCHMIDT'S PAVILION,
North Point Road 8 Miles from the City,
bloding on Boar Creek, with Fishing
Shore and Pleasure Grounds. Fish,
Crabs and all other luxuries served in
Season in the best Style and at the
Shortest Notice. A liberal patronage
solicited. Jno. Schmidt, Proprietor.

Manufacturer.

ALFRED ROSS,
[Formerly A. & D. Ross,]
Manufacturer of Crochet Needles, Eyelet
Punches, Baling and Bag Needles, Button
Hooks, Nail Punches, Cotton Hooks,
Curriers' Blades and Steels, Chisels, Oys-
ter Knives, &c. All Orders sent by Mail
will be Promptly Attended to.
White House, Chases Station P. O., P. W. and
B. R. R., Baltimore Co. Md.

Plasterer.

WM. H. RUSSELL,
Gardener and Plasterer,
Chases Station.

Teacher.

C. T. SHAFFER,
Chases Station.

EAST PART OF
TWELFTH DISTRICT.

Scale 2 Inches = to a Mile.

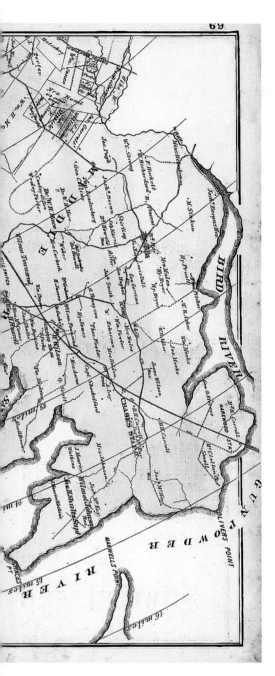

Map of east part of twelfth election district of Baltimore County, 1877, showing locations of gunning clubs

$225. James Bond, clerk of the Superior Court for Baltimore City, leased gunning privileges at Day's Point for $200 for the first season, from October 10, 1886, to April 10, 1887, with the privilege of renewing them for five additional seasons at a rental of $250 per season. The San Domingo Farm Club, a group of wealthy New York sports, paid John Cadwalader $2,000 annually for the gunning shore they leased from him on the Gunpowder River, north of Maxwell's Point. That lease included Dove's Cove or Dove's Farm, a 200-acre farm located about five miles from Magnolia near Maxwell's Point, which John Cadwalader had purchased in 1881 for $4,725. The club rented these gunning shores from John Cadwalader from 1883 to 1895. In 1886, the club had twelve members, some from New York and others from Maryland, and controlled about five miles of waterfront on the Gunpowder Neck—two on the Gunpowder River and three on the Bush River. Correspondence between Cadwalader and Charles H. Raymond, the presiding officer of the club, reveals polite and careful negotiations for the gunning rights. On May 20, 1891, John Cadwalader wrote to Charles Raymond:

> I had determined not to rent the shooting on my property again as my eldest son is now 17 years old and his brother though but ten is fond of his gun. But as their opportunities during school and college days for shooting are still very limited, I may be able to meet your wishes if any mode of doing so is acceptable. I must retain the house at Maxwells, I require it for myself and family who like to go there at any time they wish. But with your Club House at St. Domingo and including all of the privileges heretofore leased to you there and at Dove's Cove I can authorize Duck shooting on the Bar and Blinds at Maxwell's with Sundricks and Waterson's creeks for not more than four guns with the privilege of partridge shooting for not more than two guns on any one day over the whole estate. I desire to reserve the right for myself and sons or friends not exceeding three guns however at any time for both the Duck shooting at Maxwells and the creeks and also the partridge shooting. I do not expect this to be a practical interference to any great extent as for some years there will be few opportunities for us, and of course we should avoid embarrassing you.

The San Domingo Farm Club was one of the wealthiest gunning clubs, and the clubhouse at Magnolia was comfortably outfitted to permit stays of one or two weeks by club members. It was a three-story frame building containing many commodious rooms with high ceilings and large open fireplaces with fancy mantels. The rooms were filled with antique furniture, imported carpets, animal skin scatter rugs, fine oil paintings, and guns in racks and cabinets. The Harford County assessor's schedule of personal property for the San Domingo Club in 1902 included 495 books and 45 photo-prints and pictures as well as a significant amount of furniture, rugs, and decorative items. The 1896 schedule included 4 boats, 500 decoy ducks, 6 decoy swans, 2 large carriages, 24 ducking guns, fishing tackle, and a club wagon.

The accommodations and operation of the club were described in an article in the *Baltimore County Union* on April 10, 1886:

The Spesutia Island Rod and Gun Club was formed by a group of wealthy New Yorkers. Their clubhouse, set on 600 acres of the island, was valued at $10,000 in 1896.

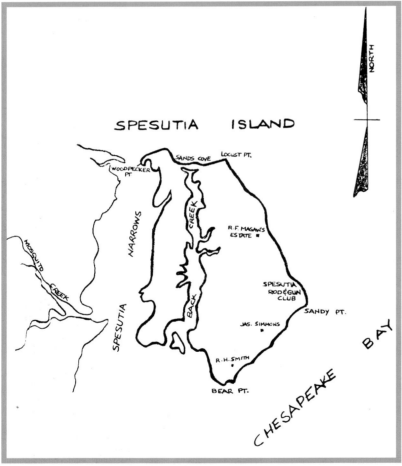

DRAWN BY ROGER J. COLBURN, 1984, BASED ON A MAP BY SIMON J. MARTENET, 1878.

No doubt they are far in advance of any similar club on the Chesapeake or its tributaries in point of outfit, comforts, accommodations, available shooting points and extent of water front. Their club-house, which is located about two hundred yards from the beach, is of ample dimensions, and admirably fitted up internally. During the gunning season they keep three house servants. They also employ three experienced gunners (who understand the habits and nature of wild fowl) to assist them in placing decoys, managing boats, dogs, etc.

The wealthy and well-connected membership often entertained prominent guests at their clubhouse. In March 1886, President Cleveland spent the weekend at San Domingo, "trying his skill at winging the famous Chesapeake bay fruit," reported the *Maryland Journal* (Towson) on April 3, 1886.

Two tracts that lay adjacent to the Cadwalader estate but were never part of it were the Philadelphia Ducking Club and Hurst family acreage. The Philadelphia Ducking Club (sometimes called the Philadelphia Gunning Club) owned a 144-acre tract in the northeastern portion of the Gunpowder peninsula, fronting on the Bush River south of King's Creek, just north of O'Possum Hollow. The club's interest in the Gunpowder Neck began in 1851 when Benjamin W. Ingersoll, Samuel B. Thomas, and James C. Fisher, all gentlemen from Philadelphia, purchased the tract from Salathial Legoe, William Taylor, and Priscilla Roberts. An unusual reservation appears in the deed: "to the heirs of Joseph Gafford, some rights to a certain point or shooting ground commonly known as The Beach at the mouth of said creek called King's Creek." The club occupied a large three-story clubhouse that overlooked the Bush River and, in 1896, owned 300 decoys. The club leased additional gunning shores from the Cadwaladers.

Benjamin Jeffers, shoreman and keeper at the San Domingo Farm Club

The Hurst family hunted from their land to the south, at Lego's Point, a 261-acre tract that they purchased in 1887 for $10,000. In *The Story of the Gunpowder Neck,* Captain Harry W. Spraker described the Hurst accommodations: "The large clubhouse contained many rooms with open fireplaces. There were also a number of fine stable and carriage houses, and a kennel of pure-bred registered Chesapeake Bay retrievers." Their rig of decoys numbered 600. The Hursts rented an additional ducking point, Sandy Point, from the Cadwaladers.

FRANK LESLIE'S ILLUSTRATED NEWSPAPER

Entered according to Act of Congress, in the year 1891, by the JUDGE PUBLISHING COMPANY, in the Office of the Librarian of Congress at Washington.—Entered at the Post-office, New York, N. Y., as Second-class Matter.

No. 1857.—VOL. LXXII.]   NEW YORK—FOR THE WEEK ENDING APRIL 18, 1891.   [PRICE, 10 CENTS. $4.00 YEARLY. 13 WEEKS, $1.00

PRESIDENT HARRISON DUCK-SHOOTING AT BENGIES, MARYLAND.—PHOTO TAKEN BY H. M. HOWE, OF PHILADELPHIA.—[SEE PAGE 188.]

FRANK LESLIE'S ILLUSTRATED NEWSPAPER

APRIL 18, 1891.]

In the blind waiting for game.

A miss.

The President's first shot.

Trophies of the second day.

The club-house.

At the close of the first day.

PRESIDENT HARRISON DUCK-SHOOTING AT BENGIES, ON CHESAPEAKE BAY.—FROM PHOTOS BY H. M. HOWE.—[SEE PAGE 188.]

At the head of the Bush River, the Bartlett-Hayward Company of Baltimore, an iron foundry owned by Thomas J. Hayward and Edward L. Bartlett, purchased four farms in the 1880s, Cedar Grove, Oak Grove, Riverside, and Tapler's Bar. All were located on the Bush River and were used as ducking shores. Bartlett, Hayward, and their guests shot at Gum Point, Fairview Point, the Water Fence in a cove near Riverside and Monk's Creek. Cedar Grove, Riverside, and Tapler's Bar had well-furnished clubhouses. The Bartlett-Hayward Company also owned the steam yacht *Comfort,* which was stationed on the Susquehanna Flats as a mother ship to their sinkbox rig. The *Comfort* was a 110-foot paddle steamer built and launched in Baltimore in 1887.

On the Bay side of the Bush River Neck at the mouth of Romney Creek lies Taylor's Island, which was purchased from the Bartlett-Hayward group in 1889 by the Taylor's Island Ducking and Fishing Club of Baltimore. The Taylor's Island Club, which was incorporated in 1889, later purchased an additional shore tract across Romney Creek at Locust Point.

Northeast of the Gunpowder Neck, at the mouth of the Susquehanna River, lies Spesutia Island. The *Harford County Democrat* of November 7, 1879, reported, "All the ducking shores about Spesutia have been rented to clubs formed of gentlemen from New York and elsewhere outside of this State." In 1886, a group of sportsmen from New York and New Jersey incorporated the Eildon Ducking Club, formed, according to its constitution, "to lease, use, and enjoy the shooting and fishing privileges of a certain property located on Spesutia Narrows in the County of Harford." They leased the Eildon Farm, on the Bush River Neck across Spesutia Narrows from Spesutia Island. They gunned from the shore and from their vessels, the *Widgeon, Maxwell, Sadie,* and *Champion.* Their enjoyment is apparent from the entry of Pennington M. Day on February 18, 1891, in the *Eildon Ducking Club Journal:* "Mr. and Mrs. P. M. Day arrived 4:45 P.M. Walked down to the water with Mr. Cole. Found 600 black heads in Briar Point Cove. We were very careful not to scare them. Returned to house with glorious anticipations, and waited patiently for the dawning of the morning. Found them still there. We put out the decoys and they returned in such multitudes that I was nearly paralyzed."

The multitudes of wildfowl were not sufficient for some sportsmen. The Bel Air *Aegis and Intelligencer* of January 1, 1892, reported that Bartlett and Hayward were stocking their shooting preserves at Cedar Grove, on the Bush River, with a shipment of live quail from Tennessee. The article further noted that the preserves were already stocked with other game and that Bartlett expected the place in two years to be well stocked with thousands of game, including German pheasants and hares.

New Yorkers predominated on Spesutia Island. In the latter part of the nineteenth century, one of the largest landowners on the island was the Spesutia Island Rod and Gun Club. In 1890, the club, which was incorporated in New York and had a membership from that state, purchased the 1,700-acre Upper Island Farm on Spesutia Island. Included in its membership were representatives of the Auchincloss, Maxwell, and Post families. The club purchased additional acreage after this first acquisition but also leased from Robert H. Smith, the owner of the Lower Island Farm, the exclusive gunning privileges "for Ducks, Geese, Swan, Birds and all other kinds of wild game from the shore and upon his land" for many years. The lease further authorized the building of a gunning box or boxes and a house. The club maintained a beautiful clubhouse, a steam yacht, and all of the accoutrements required by a first-class club. They traveled to their gunning shore by rail or on an 85-foot cutter, *Katrina,* belonging to the Auchinclosses. Indeed, "a safe harbor for yachts" was an advertised feature of Wilton Farm near Havre de Grace when that property, containing "every facility for a Ducking Club," was offered for sale in 1878.

In the Upper Bay area known as the Susquehanna Flats, many wealthy sports gunned from "floating club houses," such as the *Reckless,* a 62-foot sloop yacht built in Havre de Grace in 1880 for Henry D. Polhemus of New York and captained by William E. Moore. The Isle of Wight Club gunned from Captain Len Hamilton's sailing yacht *Nautiless* and used his rig of sinkboxes and decoys. Other gunning scows operating on the Susquehanna Flats were the *Rough Ashlar,* the *Susquehanna,* the *Lilly,* the

A Few Lines Dropped to Jeffers Shoreman and Keeper at the San Domingo Ducking Shore January 24 1897

WHEN the creeks begin to open and the ducks begin to fly,
  Dr. Wight will get your letter, to the ducking shore he'll hie.
  He's an all-around duck-shooter; a photographer to boot;
  And catches in the negative the ducks he doesn't shoot.

And Mass'r George, he'll hie, too; he's another all-arounder—
Hits every duck that passes; if she flies away, " confound her ! "
He hits 'em in the air, on the ice or in the water,
And if they don't fall dead it ain't because they hadn't oughter.

Sewert Robell, who's the all-aroundest Sport that we have got,
Killed four-and-sixty blackbirds at a single double shot.
He also shot a duck that made another Sport feel bitter,
For dead she fell and never knew which Sport it was that hit her.

And Master Rob Macbirdie is a crack-a-jack to shoot
At canvasback and widgeon, at mallard and at coot.
He'll blaze away at every duck, no matter what the distance,
And then no matter what he hits he'll say he never missed once.

And Monsieur Le Beau Louis at ducking is a teaser :
The way he shoots to kill them, kills them dead as Julius Cæsar.
The reason why so many ducks are still alive to-day,
Is simply because Louis does not always shoot that way !

AND finally " the Colonel " will come, tardy, to the blind
  To teach the boys a lesson and to beat them—in his mind.
  He shoots a Greener " Wildfowl " and always hits the game
  " A charge to keep " he gives it, but it goes off all the same.

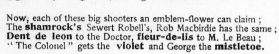

Now, each of these big shooters an emblem-flower can claim ;
The **shamrock's** Sewert Robell's, Rob Macbirdie has the same ;
Dent de leon to the Doctor, **fleur=de=lis** to M. Le Beau ;
" The Colonel " gets the **violet** and George the **mistletoe.**

A. N. from Philadelphia will also haste to march ;
His flower's the **water lily** and his smile is sweetly arch.
'Twas rumored that he shot a swan and now he takes it hard,
Because they say his only swan was only a canard.

The General from Albany's another of the cracks
With sixty ruddy ducks a day and scores of canvasbacks.
La Marguerite his flower is, the peach it is his fruit—
A clingstone for a stayer and a daisy for to shoot !

The Judge will come for Sunday, and will gravely in his seat sit :
He never shoots the foolish duck but very wisely eats it.
Valisneria is his flower and the canvasback his fare,
And should the duck be overdone, Je-whilkins ! but he'll swear.

To teach the boys a lesson

And Doctor Gustus (**primrose**) says that he will join the crew ;
He makes no bluff at shooting ducks, but he can eat a few.
And so, then, Keeper Jeffers, we will be there bye and **bye,**
When the creeks begin to open and the ducks begin to fly.

Knights of Labor, the *Widgeon,* the *James G. Blaine,* the *Mollie Burns,* the *Champion,* and the *John A. Russell.* These scows were well equipped to meet the needs of the sport gunners.

On the North East River just south of Charlestown, Cecil County, the Seneca Point Club in 1875 purchased a 145-acre tract on which was a substantial residence built in 1837 by James Hasson of Cecil County. While the club was incorporated in Maryland, at least some of the members were from Philadelphia. The residence became their clubhouse, and they gunned for ducks and geese from their property. The Wellwood Club of Cecil County owned waterfront property in Charlestown on the North East River and occupied a clubhouse there. Grover Cleveland reportedly gunned from that shore. Another gunning club in the Upper Bay was the Locust Point Gunning Club of Oakington. The Oakington estate was reputed to have one of the best gunning shores at the head of the Bay for canvasback ducks.

Crossing over the Gunpowder into Baltimore County, numerous gunning clubs also thrived in the numerous coves and broad rivers that compose the shoreline of eastern Baltimore County. Located on the Gunpowder River and Salt Petre Creek, Grace's Quarter Ducking Club, one of the Cadwalader family's Baltimore County gunning shores, contained 610 acres, including a long strip of land on the shoreline of the Gunpowder River almost opposite their Harford County shores. Another Cadwalader property was Marshy Point. Its approximately 300 acres jutted out between Salt Petre and Dundee Creeks. General George Cadwalader sold this gunning shore to Alexander Brown of Baltimore on June 2, 1862. The Brown family had occupied the property as early as 1854, pursuant to a lease, and maintained this wonderful property for sport until 1922. On April 17, 1922, the heirs of Alexander Brown sold Marshy Point to Harry C. Weiskittel and Daisy M. Weiskittel. It has remained the Weiskittel

A view of the Maxwell's Point clubhouse with a Chesapeake retriever and two other bird dogs on the front lawn

property continuously since that time. The Marshy Point Ducking Club journal dated 1854 to 1884 includes these names:

Alex. D. Brown	Wm. Gilmor
Gen. Geo. Stewart Brown	T. Harris Hodges
Issac Freeman	Francis Cooke
J. Lee Carroll	Wilmont Johnson
Col. Chas. Carroll	Wm. Hoffman
Harry Carroll	Capt. Kane
H. Oelrichs	Dr. A. Tyson
Jacob Brandt	Wm. Denison
Rob J. Lehr	Wm. Williams
J. B. Morris	Wm. Young
Wm. Sperry	Otho H. Williams
Frank Sullivan, Treasurer	James H. Barney
Wm. Graham Bowdoin	Thomas C. Harris
J.J. Sullivan	Dr. J. H. Thomas
Dr. Chas. H. Tilghman	T.N. Lee
John Stewart	Capt. Wm. Graham

To the east of Marshy Point was the clubhouse at Bengies Quarters, which is most famous for being another president's favorite gunning shore. While President Cleveland was enjoying the shooting at San Domingo, his successor (and predecessor), President Benjamin Harrison, frequented and became an honorary member of the Bengies Ducking Club. The press coverage of his excursions to that shore is delicious in detail! The *Baltimore American* of March 10 and 11, 1891, covered one of Harrison's visits in great detail. The president traveled to Bengies Quarters by private rail car:

Mr. E.C. Knight, one of the oldest members of the club, went to Washington yesterday morning from Philadelphia, and escorted the President and Senator Sewell to the shore. . . .

North shore of Maxwell's Point

A reception room at Maxwell's Point

John Cadwalader (*left*), wearing his gum boots, seated on a bench at Maxwell's Point with "old Mr. Rembold," who lived on a Cadwalader farm on Gunpowder Neck

General Manager H. F. Kenny's private car, No. 21, was sent from Philadelphia to Washington yesterday morning. The presidential party boarded the car in the B. & P. depot, and it was attached to the Philadelphia express which left at 2:10 P.M. The run to this city was made in an hour. At Union Station the private car was detached, and engine No. 113, Engineer Henry D. Plummer and Stoker Charles D. Carr, of this city, was put on. As soon as the express train pulled out of the station and was far enough ahead, the special went on, reaching Bengies at ten minutes to four o'clock.

The President was the first to leave the car. . . . He clasped hands with several gentlemen on the platform, and got into a dayton wagon with Senator Sewell and Mr. Knight, and were driven by J. P. Jones to the ducking shore, a distance of three miles, in seventeen minutes. The reporters and the President's body guard and guns tagged on behind. The road was very muddy and heavy, and when the tail end of the presidential party arrived the President was nearly ready for the blind.

The president did not waste any time before engaging in the sport he had reportedly been longing for:

In a half an hour after his arrival the President and Senator Sewell were ready for sport, and, accompanied by Preston, the steward of the club, started for the main point, where a gun in the hands of one of Preston's sons—Jerome—was making the welkin ring. The old Chesapeake bay dog Cleveland frisked and frolicked around the President as if there was no difference in politics or names, and the President patted the dog's head and said: "Good dog! Good dog! What are the prospects?" The dog whined, wagged his tail, and, like a sensible animal, held his tongue, for the reporters were around.

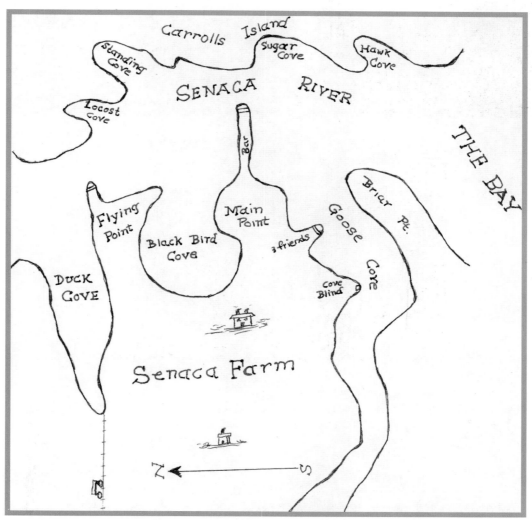

BASED ON A NINETEENTH-CENTURY ORIGINAL AT THE MARYLAND HISTORICAL SOCIETY

A tenant house at Maxwell's Point. The long bench is covered with decoys.

Although President Harrison did not have much success in shooting that afternoon, he was admirably outfitted for the occasion:

> The President wore a heavy suit of light-colored cloth. The coat was cut like a short newmarket, double-breasted and rolling collar. Instead of the regulation corduroy cap, he had a large light slouch, the crown pushed all the way up, and his legs were encased in gum boots, which came to the knee. Senator Sewell had on a regular ducking suit and gum boots. The beautiful Le Fevre gun, 12 bore, which the President has never used before at Bengies, was carried by Preston. It is a beauty, and must have cost a pretty price. It is gold-chased, and a fine piece. The party remained in the blind for a while, but the rain came down so hard and the mist was so thick that the decoys could not be seen, and darkness coming on they adjourned to the house, where a bright fire and good cheer awaited them.

Home from a hunt on Maxwell's Point

After a disappointing day in the blind, the party returned to a menu of "Green turtle soup, Southdown mutton, baked ham, white potatoes, peas, macaroni, rice, tomatoes, several salads, cranberry sauce and currant jelly and other nice things," all prepared by Aunt Emmeline, the stewardess of the ducking shore, but they had *no* ducks.

The hunter's luck was little better the next day:

> [The ducks] were all in a bunch and came down on the wind. The President heard their noise and was ready to drop a brace or two. They came and he shot—both barrels—bang! bang! and one poor little red-head fell. Jerome Preston, who was attending the blind, got in his boat to hunt the bird. When he got

Annie Oakley takes a shot at a passing duck from a grass blind on Maxwell's Point.

The April 8, 1896, entry in the Maxwell's Point journal

to the place where it fell the duck could not be found. It had only been winged and had dived and effected an escape. The President laughed and said that he hoped for better luck next time. The next time did not come during the day. A stiff north-west wind blew all the time and all the ducks sought a sheltered shore. A great rick, perhaps a quarter of a mile long, stretched along just outside of range of the blind all day, and another was seen near Carroll's Island.

Carroll's Island, perhaps the most celebrated ducking ground on the Chesapeake, lies farther east, running for about one mile, dividing the Gunpowder River from the Chesapeake Bay. It is also bounded by Seneca and Salt Petre Creeks. It consists of approximately 1,200 acres that were granted to Dr. Charles Carroll in 1746, and it remained in the Carroll family until 1822. The island was first leased to and then purchased by Colonel William Slater, who continued to lease the shooting privileges. The *Baltimore American* of September 19, 1846, reported that a fire on this "delightful island" had destroyed a farmhouse that had just been rented to a club of gentlemen from Baltimore for the purpose of gunning and fishing. On October 15, 1858, Enoch Pratt, the treasurer of the Carroll's Island Ducking Club, paid to William Slater the sum of $1,500 "for gunning privileges to Carroll Island Ducking Club for one year in advance." Officially formed in 1851, the club was limited to fifteen members and included lawyers, a doctor, and successful merchants. Of the locally prominent, in addition to Enoch Pratt, Charles Ridgely of Hampton was a member. In 1880, a new club, of twenty members, was formed and the island was purchased from the Slater estate for $30,000, each member contributing $2,500 for his share in the club. The clubhouse was expanded and refurbished, blinds were rebuilt, and it became a model club, known to sportsmen all over the country. The game books and records of this famous club have survived and allow a glimpse into the members' world.

"Sunday February 21st 1892. Saw poor Mrs. Lynch. Drove to Lego's point & Rouse Farm— Engaged Gowan to take Lynch's place." After Edward Lynch's death, Frank Gowan served as gamekeeper at Maxwell's Point until the club's takeover by the government in 1918 for creation of the Edgewood Arsenal.

Nov. 7, 1891, A. Higgins

First the Clubhouse and all the surroundings in elegant order, thanks to our very efficient "executive"—weather fine but as to "duck shooting"!!! Alas! Alas! Killed 5 woodcock in the swamps—

February 12, 1884

From 8th to 12th Rain & fog above—drifting ice & mud below. Occasional bunches of ducks wandering about without defined purposes except to avoid being shot at—Mr. Higgins & Mr. Barnes leave today having exhausted the library & worn out the cards. Too much weather—

March 4, 1884

Wind N.W. to W. intensely Cold—Ther. 14°—good many ducks moving looking for chances to feed—thought so little of appearance—laid abed until sun up—had breakfast—went to the Bar [protruding piece of land]—killed 2 canvas backs—seeing large rick of ducks under Weir Point, went over after midday meal put out decoys with the effect of starting all the ducks up the river—accordingly went back to the Bar & had a very enjoyable afternoon—killing 23 good ducks—day ends cold.

The ducks weren't the only source of excitement. On March 9, 1888, J. Olney Norris of Baltimore reported on a fire in the clubhouse:

At 1 o'clock Capt. Penny came out of his sitting room & reported the *House on Fire.* Sure enough *things* in the wall & chimney of our dining room, & Capt. Penny's sitting room were in a good blaze; *all hands* were quickly on the spot & not excited (except the woman cook) after cutting away the mantle & lath work in "Penny's room" & the wash board in "Potter's" room above, with pails of water applied with a *dipper* & *over hand,*-we succeed in putting out the Fire;- had the stove in the dining room removed, to examine things thoroughly,-*all safe* for the night;-shall send carpenter & stove man to repair damage, and duly notify Insurance Companies to Pony Up!! J. O. Norris

Thomas F. Cadwalader and his bird dogs

Farther south, the Bowley's Quarters Gunning Club occupied a portion of a tract of 822 acres with nine miles of shoreline. In November 1854, the approximately 400-acre farm known as Bowley's Quarters was advertised for sale in the *Baltimore American* as a place "celebrated as one of the very best locations for shooting Ducks and for Fishing, being bounded by Middle River and Seneca River. It offers a rare opportunity to Ducking or Sporting Clubs for a purchase."

The Seneca Ducking Club was located nearby. Its members purchased Seneca Farm in 1852 and the clubhouse was built in the summer of 1853. The earliest Seneca logbook describes the location of the Seneca Farm as being bounded on the north by Duck Cove, on the south by Goose Cove, on the east by Carroll's Island, and on the west by Bowley's Quarters. This logbook also contains a hand-drawn map of the 100-acre Seneca Farm which locates the mansion house, Cove Blind on Goose Point, Box Blind on Main Point, and Flying Point at the mouth of Seneca Creek. The report of the hunters' guns resounded great distances along the undeveloped shores of the Upper Chesapeake. On October 29, 1856, a member of the Seneca Club reported: "Considerable shooting direction of Back River &

Walter Chrysler, automobile pioneer, and Albanus Phillips at Bishops Head Gun Club in 1936

Townsend. Not a gun fired at Carroll's Island or vicinity this day. Thousands of ducks bedded this afternoon in Sugar Cove, opposite us." Townsend, also known as Cuckold's Point, was just opposite Miller's Island. The Seneca Club maintained a boat and skiff and seventy-five decoys at Box Blind and thirty-five decoys and a skiff and oars at Cove Blind. At Flying Point, the logbook reported, "Decoys are not needed Best wind there, N. West & cold."

Numerous other ducking clubs peppered the shores of the rivers feeding the Bay. While journal and gunning logs have not survived for most of these clubs, newspaper advertisements for the sale of these properties reveal the extent to which the sport of wildfowl shooting was enjoyed up and down the Chesapeake. In Baltimore County, the Biddisons maintained a shore at Log Point on Middle River, and Bull Neck Farm included five miles of shoreline on that river and on Stansbury Creek and a comfortable frame clubhouse. Another club on Middle River was the Planters Point Ducking Club, which enjoyed exceptionally good early fall and spring duck shooting and a large and commodious, beautifully furnished, and excellently equipped clubhouse. On Back River, the land of General Tobias Stansbury and his son Carville S. Stansbury contained well-known ducking shores, and clubs were also located at Cox's Point and at the Japanese Shore. In the September 14, 1871, issue of the Baltimore *Sun,* the Japanese Shore, described as a "very valuable GUNNING POINT and FISHING SHORE" with a twelve-room mansion, was offered for sale along with "Boats, Seines, and Decoys, and all apparatus pertaining to a well regulated Farm and Gunning Shore." In a *Baltimore American* article of May 5, 1895, the facilities at Japanese Shore were described in detail:

On it there is a large clubhouse, elegantly arranged and capable of accommodating about forty people. The house is supplied with parlors, smoking-rooms, dining-rooms, a kitchen and several bedrooms. Two cooks, a waiter and an hostler are kept about the place throughout the season. The clubhouse is surrounded with large shade trees and beautiful flowers. Some distance from the clubhouse are the stables and and the carriage-house. They are large and modern, and can accommodate twenty horses and fifty-eight carriages.

Other Baltimore County gunning shores included the Miller's Island Ducking Club's, Townsend (or Cuckold's) Point on the Patapsco Neck opposite that island, and Rocky Point Farm's Balliston Point, which was pur-

DRAWN BY ROGER J. COLBURN, 1984, BASED ON A MAP BY SIMON J. MARTENET, 1878

The clubhouse of the Bishops Head Gunning Club in Dorchester County.

chased by the well-known Baltimore gunmaker, Alexander McComas, with others in 1881. McComas had been gunning from that shore since at least 1877, apparently leasing the privilege. Walnut Grove Ducking Club's shore was on Back River; a record of the ducks bagged there from 1864 to 1884 survives. Farther south were the shores of Fishing Creek Farm, outside of Annapolis, described in the Baltimore *Sun* of August 28, 1879, as the finest ducking shores on the Chesapeake.

Nineteenth-century writings make fewer references to the pursuit of wildfowl along the rivers of the Lower Eastern Shore, such as the Choptank, Nanticoke, Transquakin, and Miles, as they flow into the Bay. In fact, few records of the sport along the Lower Bay survive. We do know that the Hooper's Island Gunning Club, formed in 1896 by a group of Baltimoreans, was a significant enough presence in Dorchester County at the turn of the century that a local law was passed to protect their shooting grounds. The Bishops Head Gun Club, also in Dorchester County, did their shooting on lands known as Bloodsworth and Billy's Island, which they purchased in 1921. While rivers such as the Choptank, Nanticoke, Transquakin, and Miles provided sport, it was to a lesser extent than in the upper reaches of the Bay. Cambridge, Maryland, was full of gunners from Philadelphia and Baltimore in November of 1878, but there were more gunners than game. "Every partridge on the Peninsula [had] a man after him," observed the *Cambridge Chronicle*. The newspaper also reported on the more successful gunning along the Upper Bay that month: "Near Havre de Grace one day recently, Mr. Barns of Cecil co., killed 196 ducks. Another killed 185 and so on: until 4,000 were killed during the day, and many more would have been killed had the wind not been so high. But few ducks have as yet been killed in the Choptank this season."

The extent to which the gunning of wildfowl was pursued and the resultant value of these gunning shores are reflected in farm real estate advertisements. When the trustees of the estate of William P. Taylor of Harford County advertised the sale of his farms, among them Otter Point Farm on the Bush River, the notice of sale emphasized that the properties included "several fine GUNNING POINTS, valuable FISHING SHORES, &c. The latter are very profitable." The ad pointed out that the farms were "in close proximity to the Philadelphia, Wilmington and Baltimore Railroad, being near Edgewood Station, and they thereby afford convenient access to sportsmen and fishermen from Philadelphia and Baltimore."

The sport was not just for the very wealthy, as an announcement in the *Sun* of September 29, 1879, implies: "WANTED—A few MEMBERS for the best Ducking Shore on Middle river; terms moderate. Apply, between the hours of 7 and 9 P.M., to J. FRANK OLIVER, Graphic Cigar Store, northeast corner of Broadway and Baltimore street."

Game books, gunning logs, and journals survive from the Carroll's Island Ducking Club, the Eildon Ducking Club, the Seneca Ducking Club, the Marshy Point Ducking Club, and Maxwell's Point. Some of these journals and gunning logs provide not only a detailed account of the pursuit of the sport by the well-to-do but also insight into society in those times; they stand as a social commentary.

The slender brown leather volume entitled *Marshy Point Ducking Club 1854* provides glimpses into the social fabric. Prior to 1862 the journal is little more than a listing by date of the members who gunned at the point, the dues paid, and cryptic commentary on the harvest: "Henry Oelrichs $3.75, 13 ducks & 1 swan weighing 15lb killed at Sperry Blind." However, after Alexander Brown purchased Marshy Point in the summer of 1862, it became a place of social gathering as well. Mrs. Alexander Brown's first visit to the point was Thanksgiving 1862, when the gathering did "ample justice to a good dinner." The visitors arrived by train or carriage or boat: "July 3, 1866 The Yacht Rapidan Capt Young commanding left Balto @ 1¼ PM & arrived at Marshy Pt at 5:24 making the run from Chases Wharf in the unprecedented time of 4 hours & 9 minutes. . . . on the same afternoon F. Sullivan drove T. H. Hodges down by the road making the drive in one hour thirty minutes to the door."

Many visitors came to Marshy Point. They were entertained by their hosts, dined on delicacies, and enjoyed the camaraderie of friendship. Here are notes from the Marshy Point journal:

November 4, 1864
On the morning of the 4th the Gallant "Young" arrived with two charming Young Ladies—the Misses McRa formerly of Balto—who are to remain several days at the Lodge.

December 8, 1864
Mr. Young appeared with a wreath of evergreen around his *new* hat & of course frightened all the ducks away.

April 27, 1865
Turkeys and Eat the fried oysters. Crabes. Snipe. & the delicacies of the shooting point.

November 9, 1867
Mrs. Brown on her way to N.Y. stopped to claim a bet made with Col. Howard.

December 4, 1867
Mr. Harris made his appearance in the old coat of the late President Mr. H. Oelrichs but it was too late to shoot any ducks. Since writing a goose was seen in that same coat. Some say it was a bald pate!!!

The *Maxwell's Point Visitors' Book* was maintained from 1880 until "The End of Everything" on November 24, 1917, the day the entire Gunpowder Neck became the site of the Edgewood Arsenal, a U.S. Army installation. The visitors' book is several hundred pages of charming sketches, original poetry, and journal entries that range from brief descriptions to detailed accounts of a day at Maxwell's Point. When the Gunpowder River was frozen, the ducks couldn't land, so the occupants of Maxwell's Point engaged in other activities, as a visitors' book entry for February 21, 1895 explains: "The frozen condition of the river made our experience a unique one for Maxwell's Point. On Friday we made our return trip from Raphael Farm via the Gunpowder on foot and on Saturday we skated to Day's Point and back. We ate several times a day with the consequent torpor."

The Cadwaladers, owners of Maxwell's Point, often gathered at the point for Thanksgiving and returned during the Christmas season. The visitors' book provides this account of part of one such visit:

December 28, 1900
Mr. C, T.F.C. & J.C. Jr. & Dr. W. H. Jr. arrived, spent their energies immediately on the pleasing task of preparing the Christmas Tree. An even prettier effect than usual was produced and new glass ball ornaments substituted for the time-honored paper fishes and gew-gaws of former days. Francis outdid himself in amassing presents & we were able to supply every kid with a plethora of horns, dolls, mouth organs and other instruments to torture their parent's ears with. The clanging of the big bell summoned the clans together & they came up from Gowan's like a small army, the boys lined up in front, then the little girls, followed by the half-growns & staid matrons. . . . After the Tree, the usual cake & wine were handed out by the Governor [the family patriarch] and the health of the New Century was drunk without much apparent emotion. Every farm with Children on it was represented with the exception of the Edgewood.

The entry of December 31, 1900, contained a wish that was not to be granted: "The Nineteenth Century has only 5 ½ hours more of life as I say farewell to the Point once more. May the old place remain during the twentieth as it has up to this time! T.F.C. [Thomas Francis Cadwalader]."

Shooting Methods

O F THE VARIOUS methods used to kill waterfowl in the past, several required decoys while others did not. All of the gunning decoys known today were carved for use with sinkboxes, bushwhack boats, or in point shooting with decoys. Point shooting, pass shooting, and bar shooting could be accomplished without decoys. Toling for ducks incorporated the aid of a playful dog as a device to lure the fowl.

TOLING

All of the early waterfowling histories go to great lengths to describe toling for ducks. Although extensively practiced upon the Chesapeake by the beginning of the nineteenth century, it was not exclusive to the region. According to *The American Shooter's Manual,* published in Philadelphia in 1872, toling was employed in most of the states on the eastern seaboard. In 1845, J. S. Skinner described toling in his work *The Dog and the Sportsman,* noting that this method of shooting fowl had its origin near Havre de Grace, Maryland, soon after 1800. One tradition suggests that this method came about from the observations of a duck hunter. The hunter, waiting in his blind for a shot, observed a fox playing along the shore. The antics of the fox attracted the flock of wildfowl bedded on the water to within shooting range. Having witnessed this, early fowlers trained small dogs with the specific intent of "toling," or enticing, the birds. They preferred small dogs, preferably bushy-tailed and red in color. These dogs were trained from puppyhood to run after small sticks or pebbles that were thrown along the shore by the hunter or his partner; the dogs would ignore the fowl offshore and focus on the thrown objects.

Harry Harewood's *A Dictionary of Sports; or, Companion to the Field, the Forest, and the River Side,* published in London in 1835, suggests that toling originated in England. The dog was employed in attracting fowl by "teaching him playful ways," which "brings him as it were to amuse the [live] decoys." The birds "then not only become used to his gambols, but delight in them, and will dash after his tricks whenever they are exhibited." The disturbance created by the dogs is "made use of to rouse the lethargic and sleepy habit" of the ducks, which then "fly to the dog to scare him away from disturbing their quiet repose."

Shooting canvasback ducks, from *Harper's Weekly,* January 9, 1875

Some species of waterfowl toled easily and some not at all. Canvasbacks, redheads, and bluebills were the easiest to tole. Skinner described canvasbacks as having their heads raised and a "kind of idiotic look in the eye" when they were within shooting range and redheads as appearing "unconscious," with their heads "tucked," on their approach to the shore. Incidents were reported in which the fowl would take no notice of a toling dog but would swim immediately to the sight of a red silk handkerchief tied to the end of the fowler's ramrod. The earliest accounts reveal that perhaps some of the dog's interest in this sport was based on his reward in a share of the day's ducks. Skinner commented that he had often divided the day's game with his dog.

The first shot at the birds was made while they were still resting on the water, while the second occurred as the birds rose from the water in fright. The proper and most destructive moment to shoot the ducks was when they presented a side view. W. Mackay Laffan, author of "Canvas-Back and Terrapin," which appeared in 1883 in *Sport with Gun and Rod in American Woods and Waters,* vividly describes the "sport" of toling:

> Cold Spring was full of ducks, but they were all "bedded" far out from the shore. We made for a sheltered cove, and were shortly crawling on our hands and knees through the calamus and dry, yellow-tufted marsh-grass, which made

FACING PAGE
Part of an article about duck shooting from *American Agriculturist,* 1868

Fig. 1.—INLET ON CHESAPEAKE BAY.

Fig. 2.—SHOOTING FROM A BLIND OR SCREEN.

Duck Shooting.

In October the various species of ducks arrive from the North, and congregate in the bays along the coast, where they find their favorite feeding grounds. Chesapeake Bay and its tributaries have long been famous for the immense flocks of wild fowl which resort to them at this

ite food of the Canvas-backs is the Tape-grass or Eel-grass, *Vallisneria spiralis*. This, which, by the way, is not a grass at all, has flat, tape-like leaves, two feet or more in length, and grows in slow streams, completely submerged. It is said that the Canvas-backs eat only the roots of this plant, while other ducks feed upon the leaves. The superiority of this species of

seems to be conceded that the excellence of the Canvas-back is due to the Vallisneria, and this relationship is recognized in the specific scientific name, the bird being called *Anas Vallisneria*. Duck shooting calls for the display of strategy, and those who follow it for sport or for profit resort to various ingenious expedients to get near the game. One of our artists sends

Fig. 3.—TOLING FOR DUCKS.

Fig. 4.—MASKED BOAT.

season, and have become especially noted as the resort of the Canvas-back, generally esteemed the most delicious of all ducks. In our markets, when the Canvas-backs bring four dollars a pair, other kinds are sold for a dollar or less. The ducks when they arrive from the North are very poor, but they rapidly fatten after reaching their feeding grounds. The favor-

duck is attributable to this particular food, which is in the Chesapeake called "Wild Celery," though it has no resemblance to celery, nor is it botanically related to it. A gentleman from Albemarle Sound informed us that Canvas-backs were abundant in those waters, but as they were without their proper food, "Wild Celery," they were less esteemed than some other species. It

us sketches he has taken in Chesapeake Bay, which illustrate some of the methods of hunting. Certain favored spots over which the birds pass as they fly from one feeding place to another are often rented at a high rate as shooting grounds. A point of this kind is shown in figure 1. Blinds or screens are built to hide the sportsmen who lie in wait for the birds. A nearer

Fig. 5.—SHOOTING FROM FLOAT.

Fig. 6.—NIGHT SHOOTING.

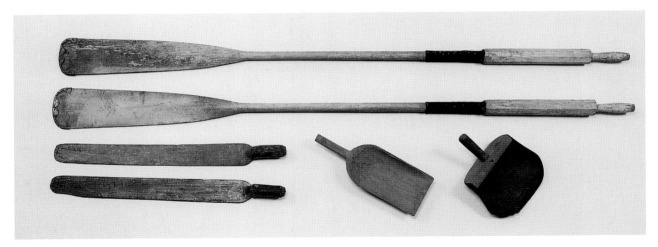

Items used at Spesutia Island for night gunning

Live goose decoys in their pen, January 1917

a good cover almost to the water's edge. Joe left the dogs with us, and, going back into the woods, presently returned with his hat full of chips from the stump of a tree that had been felled. The ducks were swimming slowly up before the wind, and it seemed possible that a large body of them might pass within a few hundred yards of where we were. The two dogs, Rollo and Jim, lay down close behind us, and Joe, lying flat behind a thick tuft a few yards to our right, and about fifteen feet from the water's edge, had his hat full of chips and held the young spaniel beside him. All remained perfectly quiet and watched the ducks. After nearly three-quarters of an hour's patient waiting, we saw a large body of ducks gradually drifting in toward our cove. They were between three and four hundred yards away, when B. said: "Try them now, Joe! Now boys, be ready, and don't move a muscle until I say fire!"

Once the ducks moved closer, the toling began:

Then Joe commenced tolling the ducks. He threw a chip into the water, and let his dog go. The spaniel skipped eagerly in with unbounded manifestations of delight. I thought it for a moment a great piece of carelessness on Joe's part. But in went another chip just at the shallow edge, and the spaniel entered into the fun with the greatest zest imaginable. Joe kept on throwing his chips, first to the right and then to the left, and the more he threw, the more gayly the dog played. For twenty minutes I watched this mysterious and seemingly purposeless performance, but presently, looking toward the ducks, I noticed that a few coots had left the main body and had headed toward the dog. Even at that distance, I could see that they were attracted by his actions. They were soon followed by other coots, and, after a minute or two, a few large ducks came out from the bed and joined them. Others followed these, and then there were successive defections of rapidly increasing numbers. Several ducks stood up in the water by the aid of their wings, sustained themselves a moment, and, sitting down, swam rapidly around in involved circles, betraying the greatest excitement. And still the dog played, and played, and gamboled in graceful fashion after Joe's chips. By this time the ducks were not over two hundred yards away, and, taking heart of their numbers, were approaching rapidly, showing in all their actions the liveliest curiosity. It was an astonishing and most interesting spectacle to see them marshaling about, to see long lines stand up out of the water, to note their fatuous excitement, and the fidelity with which the dog kept to his deceitful antics, never breaking the spell by a fatal bark or a disturbing movement. The more wildly he played, the more erratic grew the actions of the ducks. They deployed from right to left, retreated and advanced, whirled in companies, and crossed and recrossed one another. Stragglers hurried up from the rear, and bunches from the main bed came fluttering and pushing through

Henry H. Boyer and his father-in-law, Joshua Columbus Watts, hold John Payhill's big gun after its confiscation, circa 1906.

Shooting Methods ❁ 31

to the front to see what it was all about. By this time the nearest skirmishers were not a hundred yards off, and as Joe threw the chips to right or left and the dog wheeled after them, so would the ducks immediately wheel from side to side. On they came until some were about thirty yards away. These held back, while the ungovernable curiosity of those behind made them push forward until the dog had a closely packed audience of over a thousand ducks gathered in front of him.

"Fire!" said B., and the spectacle ended in havoc and slaughter. We gave them the first barrel sitting, and, as they rose, the second. We got thirty-nine canvasbacks and red-heads and some half dozen coots.

George Bird Grinnell, in his 1901 book *American Duck Shooting*, indicated that it was usual to get a dozen, or even twenty to twenty-five birds in a tole, but that a larger number was unusual. However, the same flock of ducks could be toled several times in the course of a day, and the slaughter was consequently often enormous. Elisha J. Lewis, in his 1855 second edition of *The American Sportsman*, recorded an incident in which the same batch of ducks was successfully decoyed "three successive times in the course of an hour, . . . slaying at each fire a large number."

According to Grinnell, the practice of toling had fallen out of favor years before, because it was so destructive and of little satisfaction to a true sportsman. Lewis noted that it was forbidden on some of the Chesapeake Bay shoreline owned by gunning clubs, although some shores on the Gunpowder and Bush Rivers were exclusively devoted to toling. Lewis disagreed with the detractors of toling, seeing nothing improper or unsportsmanlike in the practice. He commented, "This method of killing ducks is less injurious in its effects upon the movements of wildfowl than any kind

Harry Merrith and "Kaiser," January 24, 1924

Robert F. McGaw, Jr., and gunning partner placing decoys for their bushwhack rig. The decoys at the stern and to the right of the bow can be identified as canvasbacks carved by Columbus Fletcher.

of *boat-shooting* that can be practised, as it never disturbs them on their feeding grounds, but attacks them only when foolishly wandering away from their usual secure haunts."

PASS SHOOTING

Of all methods employed to shoot ducks, the most difficult, and therefore the most sportsmanlike, was pass shooting, also called bar or overhead shooting. Pass shooting is no longer practiced to any extent because of the diminished flocks. In pass shooting, the gunner positioned himself on a narrow peninsula or bar extending out into the water. To be most success-ful, he needed to be directly below the flight path of the ducks. He then shot them as they passed overhead on the way to their feeding grounds. At times, pass shooters concealed themselves behind natural rush blinds or in boxes or pits dug into the ground. Early in the season, when the birds were less wary, the gunner would oftentimes stand out in plain view of the fowl. As Frank Forester commented in his *Game In Its Seasons:* "The sport is generally enhanced by the difficulty of the shooting; and it is said that even the best of upland shots, or fowl shots, accustomed only to stooling, fail of success at first in this flight shooting, from the difficulty of calculat-ing the distance of the teams, and the rapidity of their motion."

At Carroll's Island in Baltimore County, perpendicular or overhead shooting, as they called it, was practiced for many years. Club members pursued the sport after the birds had become too wary to decoy on the points. Early in the season, 10-gauge guns were used. But, as the ducks began to fly ever higher, shooters turned to the 8-, 6-, and finally the 4-bore fowlers. The sport nevertheless remained excellent according to an article on Carroll's Island in the April 13, 1882, *Forest and Stream*. The author recounted the tale of a man who had recently in three days killed 117 canvasbacks and redheads from his point by "overhead shooting." This was considered "good sport" because, hunters observed, the ducks flew much higher over those points than they had in "olden times."

An excellent description of the experience of pass shooting on the bars at Carroll's Island appeared in an article in *Turf, Field and Farm* on March 2, 1888, and was included in *A Sporting Family of the Old South,* by Harry Worcester Smith. The shooters would position themselves in "stands," which were uncovered boxes about five feet square. The bar divided the Bay from the Gunpowder River, and over it at certain times the fowl passed in "incredible numbers." These gunning boxes would be spaced at approximately the length of a gunshot. The boxes were equipped with "a bench at either end, one serving as a seat, the other to hold the ammunition ready for rapid loading." They served not only to hide the shooter but also to provide him with some shelter from the cutting winds. Outside the boxes, on the lee side, the retrievers would anxiously await to be called into duty. Perpendicular shooting was also practiced at Maxwell's Point, a very narrow strip of land, and at Locust Point, Plumb Point, and Little and Big Welch Points on the Elk River.

Some sportsmen were especially devoted to pass shooting. In an 1891 letter from the president of the San Domingo Ducking Club, Henry Tho-

"The Esquimaux cap—an excellent cap for duck shooters with glasses to protect the eyes from wind and sleet." The ideal protection for ice hole shooters.

The Frank Lawrence grass suits to be worn when gunning for wild goose, duck, and shore birds

mas Weld, to John Cadwalader concerning the lease by the club, Weld stated: "Should you not rent the Point absolutely to a club, would you be willing to give the privilege of our club occupying 2 blinds on the bar (there are 6) during the period of the bar shooting—we going over in the morning and returning in afternoon—or even add to it Rundrin Creek. Some of us, especially I, am especially devoted to this bar shooting, and would sooner kill one overhead, than three over decoys."

In addition to ducks, other species were taken by bar shooting. The *Game Book* of the Carroll's Island Club records the following events on February 8, 1884: "Mr. Higgins killed two swan flying over the bar"; and on November 22, 1884, they recorded "a large eagle was killed on the bar."

The difficulty with bar shooting was that, while a certain portion of the birds fell at once on the bar or so near it they could be easily recovered by the dogs, others came down to water a long way off and in rough water or fog could not be retrieved.

POINT SHOOTING

"No form of duck shooting is more pleasing and none more artistic than what is termed as point shooting; and, when the weather is favorable, no form offers greater rewards," observed Grinnell in *American Duck Shooting*. Point shooting, like pass shooting, was a genuinely sportsmanlike way of shooting ducks that is generally no longer in use. The shooter would station himself on one of the many points or bars over which the ducks flew in the course to and from their feeding grounds. The success of this shooting method was dependent upon the elements. In some cases, strong winds would force the ducks to fly out of the shooting range of the points, but when wind and weather were favorable, and the fowl were flying briskly, great sport would be generated. Point shooting required the assistance of a retriever, as many ducks were usually killed.

Elisha J. Lewis made reference to premier locations for this style of shooting in *The American Sportsman*: "the points immediately about Havre de Grace, the Narrows of Spesutia, a few miles farther down, Taylor's Island, Abbey Island, Legoe's Point, Marshy Point, Bengie's Point, Robbins's and Ricket's Point[s], Maxwell's Point, and Carrol's Island," as well as "some good points about Elk and Northeast Rivers, and a few on the western shore." Frank Forester dubbed Carroll's Island the most famous of these stations.

Point shooting could also be accomplished with the employment of decoys. The decoys were anchored a short distance off of a point of land that extended into the Bay or off a river shore. From fifty to one hundred decoys were necessary for point shooting, the more the better. At certain points along the Bay, ducks were plentiful enough that decoys were unnecessary. In the Seneca Farm Club log book of 1853, an entry details the equipment required at the various shooting points. Decoys were kept at Box Blind (75 decoys), at Three Friends Point (25), and at Cove Point (35); but at Flying Point, at the mouth of Seneca Creek, the entry advised, de-

Percy Thayer Blogg shooting over decoys from the blind at Seneca Ducking Club, circa 1920

coys were not needed. In 1844, J. P. Giraud, Jr., in his book *The Birds of Long Island,* mentioned that Miller's Island, about fifteen miles from Baltimore, was a famous place for point shooting of canvasbacks and other species of ducks. Parties who engaged in duck shooting rented the points on this island for large sums. Decoys were not used, and these hunters did not engage in the unsportsmanlike practice of sailing after and harassing the ducks on their feeding grounds.

BUSHWHACKING

In this method of duck shooting, specially designed "bushwhack boats" were used to conceal hunters from their prey. These boats were painted white. A hole was cut into the stern and lined with a leather gasket; a sculling oar fit tightly through this hole. The sculler, squatting in the rear of the boat, worked the oar in such a fashion as to propel the boat forward with as little disturbance as possible to the surface of the water; in this way, the shooter was brought close to the resting flocks without notice. The shooter crouched in the bow of the boat behind a one-foot-high white canvas curtain, which extended back from both sides of the bow. These gunning boats would incorporate up to 150 decoys in their assemblage of equipment, called a rig.

GILL NETTING

A method of "harvesting" fowl that is seldom written about because it was so distasteful consisted of placing gill nets under the water on the feeding grounds. When the fowl dove for food, their heads and wings became entangled in the nets, and they were drowned. This method, fortunately not widely practiced on the waters of the Chesapeake, was successful for only short periods of time. It drove the ducks from their feeding grounds and prevented their returning for weeks. Gill netting was apparently done in Worcester County late in the nineteenth century; a law was passed in 1880 prohibiting the use of nets to capture wildfowl in that county.

NIGHT SHOOTING

Night gunning was another method of taking ducks that was not only frowned upon by most sportsmen but was frequently the subject of conservation legislation. This method relied on the devastating attraction that light has on flying birds. In the November 24, 1876, issue of the Bel Air *Aegis and Intelligencer,* a story mentioned the catastrophic impact that the lanterns of lighthouses were having on fowl in flight, particularly in April and October, during their migration: "The keeper of the new and lofty light on Anastasia Island, at St. Augustine, Fla., informed the writer that there is scarcely any dark night in the year that does not witness the destruction of numbers of birds that dash themselves against the light, and that often the number found in the morning ranges from 20 to 50. Ducks, however, are 'the most notable victims' due to the 'velocity of their flight,' and the writer estimates that 100,000 birds had been killed in this way along the Atlantic Coast the previous year."

In night gunning, the shooter would paddle into large, bedded flocks with bright lanterns called "night reflectors," which would have a mesmerizing effect on the birds. The night reflector consisted of a large reflector behind a common naphtha lamp. As described in the *Aegis and Intelligencer* of November 9, 1877, "the birds, fascinated by the light, swim to it from every side and bob against the boat in helpless confusion. The number of birds secured depends only on the caliber of the gun." However, because of the low esteem most sportsmen held for this activity, the night gunner might go away with not only a large catch but also "a charge of shot in his body from some indignant sportsman on shore." Most of the night gunning was done with large punt guns, which were mounted or swiveled in the bow of the boat. Kills of 80 to 100 ducks with one shot were not unusual. Paddling up on resting ducks with a big gun was practiced on occasion even during daylight hours.

Records of night gunning made it into the game books of local ducking clubs, where it was viewed with great disfavor. The Carroll's Island *Game Book* of November 25, 1884, recorded: "Night gunners after geese of which there are immense numbers in the coves. Firing at 7:45 and 9:15 [p.m.]." This disfavored practice was first prohibited in Harford County in 1832, when night gunning was banned by law in the waters of Swan Creek, Spesutia Narrows, Romney Creek, and the Bush and Gunpowder Rivers. Unfortunately, the practice continued for many years, due to the lack of enforcement of the law. The April 13, 1882, issue of *Forest and Stream* made the following comments:

Placing decoys at Towner's Cove on Bush River Neck, circa 1910

From *Sports Afield,* March 1893

The falling off in the quantity of ducks in the flats is unquestionably owing to the persistent, unlawful practice of night shooting with large and small guns, carried on by a few lawless men, and if permitted to continue, this will soon make wild fowl shooting about the waters of the Chesapeake a thing of the past. How strange it is that the residents of Havre de Grace and the hundreds of others who get a good living from the killing of wild fowl, do not make energetic efforts to put a stop to this villainous practice. Here are a few men, well known to those who follow the water and shooting, who are destroying the means of a large mass of people from obtaining an honest living.

ICE HOLE SHOOTING

Although the Middle Atlantic states are not at present known for their particularly fierce winters, such was not the case in Havre de Grace in the winter of 1851-52, when the ice across the Susquehanna was so thick that the railroad tracks were laid directly on the ice. Mention of this circumstance appeared in the *Baltimore Patriot* on February 12 of 1852: "The ice in the river has not changed—the thaw was but partial, and has caused so slight a rise in the river, as to leave the ice every where above as it was before. The mails, the passengers, the baggage and freight, went over the track on the ice to-day, and the prospect is they will do so for some weeks." Weather such as this necessitated extreme measures for the determined duck hunter, but the results could be rewarding. As Giraud noted in *The Birds of Long Island,* in the nineteenth century canvasback ducks were normally "vigilant and difficult to approach," but in severe weather, when their feeding grounds were frozen over, they could be "readily killed at 'air openings.'"

Shooting ducks on frozen waters was accomplished by cutting a hole in the ice directly over a favorite feeding ground or by taking advantage of naturally made openings in the ice. The hole was cut close enough to the shoreline for the shooter to be concealed in a blind within easy range of the hungry fowl. Some fowlers disguised themselves in white clothing along snow-covered shorelines.

The journal of Maxwell's Point makes note of this method of gunning in an entry for Friday, December 18, 1909: "Game thirteen ducks. Greeks frozen but we broke ice for the decoys. One crippled cygnet escaped from Thomas F. Cadwalader and Flint."

LIVE DECOYS

Wooden decoys were successful in the killing of fowl, but Mother Nature provided the best decoys, in the form of tethered, live birds. They were so successful that they, like the sinkbox, were outlawed as of the 1935 season. These live birds were commonly referred to as tollers. Many shooters maintained large pens of wildfowl, not only for their own use but also for distribution throughout the country. Ads for live decoys for sale appeared in most of the sporting magazines around the turn of the twentieth century.

Clarence Webb, Jr., of Elkton, Maryland, who gunned for geese over live decoys, shared with me his days of gunning by this method on a visit to his home in August of 1993. In 1920 he found a crippled goose and raised it as his first decoy. He was never without live decoys for the balance of his gunning days. Live decoys were pinioned (had the tips of their wings cut) before the first flight and were tethered by a leather or heavy cord harness. The tethers were attached to a forged iron peg. The birds were always tethered two to a peg. Clarence told me that the drakes made better callers. He tried to buy the best birds around; in the mid 1920s he drove to Chincoteaque to buy a bird whose reputation was widely known among goose hunters. This bird's name was "Old 66," apparently a reference to the number of fowl killed on his best day. He recalled the names of other decoys he had owned. "Bull" had been the best and loudest caller of any that he had ever owned; others were named "Doc," "Pete," and "Repeat." Clarence virtually controlled the Canada goose population on the Cecil County side of the Susquehanna Flats in the late 1920s and early 1930s. In those days, prior to the advent of the modern-day corn picker, few of these big northern neighbors rested in this region on their migratory route heading south, because the harvesting methods left less upon which they could feed. Even after legislation passed in 1934 outlawed the use of live birds, Clarence kept a flock of geese and ducks. He proudly showed me his twenty Canada geese and sixteen mallards, on what turned out to be one of my last visits to this "keeper of the fowl."

The Era of the Sinkbox

PERHAPS THE DEADLIEST of the gunning devices was the sinkbox, or sink boat. It was in use on the waters surrounding Long Island, New York, by 1838, but when it appeared in the Chesapeake region is unknown. In 1849 the Maryland legislature prohibited the sinkbox and sneak boats (bushwhack boats) in the waters of the Chester and Sassafras Rivers and the Chesapeake Bay bordering on Kent County. It was last used in Maryland on the Susquehanna Flats, prior to being outlawed forever by federal game regulations in 1935.

In 1842, in his work *Sporting Scenes and Sundry Sketches; being the Miscellaneous Writings of J. Cypress, Jr.,* Frank Forester described the Long Island "machine" or "battery" as follows: "a wooden box of the necessary dimensions to let a man lie down upon his back, just tightly fitting enough to let him rise again.—It is not unlike that box which we have all got to be shut up in, at the end of the chapter of our lives." Forester went on to describe the appropriate location for this box—in a middle bay with shallow waters where the birds have a "haunt." The battery was to be placed far from any point where, through the birds' experience, they might fear a hidden "skulker." The decoys used in conjunction with the sinkbox required "fastidious" arrangement on it. John Krider described their proper arrangement in his *Sporting Anecdotes:*

> They were placed so as to ride freely without coming in contact with each other, principally at the stern and on either hand of the side wings, the perfection of the art appearing to be to avoid leaving a gap in any part of the rank, and yet to prevent, if possible, the ducks from falling foul. A few of the lightest were placed immediately on the wings, and several heads of decoys were firmly fixed on wooden pins on the deck of the battery. The false ducks were not all imitations of canvass-backs, but had red-heads, black-heads, and a few baldpates, intermingled with the nobler variety. The outside duck at the tail of the rank was a veteran canvass-back, facetiously called the toller.

John Pusey, who was shooting from a sinkbox by 1929, told me that the Puseys favored the high-neck canvasbacks carved by Charles Nelson Barnard at the front of the decoy rig as tollers. A sinkbox rig could number from 200 to 500 decoys. In 1902, Madison Mitchell's sinkbox rig at Plum Point, Harford County, included 300 decoys, as did the rigs of the Locust Point Club of Oakington and that of J. B. Hoskins of 1201 West Fayette

Captain Billy Moore of the *Reckless* in his sinkbox at the mouth of the Bay

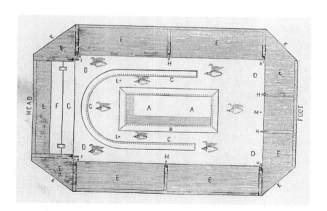

Elisha Lewis's description of the sinkbox in
The American Sportsman, 1855

Street in Baltimore. Canvasbacks, redheads, and bluebills were the most popular decoys, those species being the choicest for table fare. Ducks were in great demand for the market as well as for sport.

The first glimpse of a sinkbox would not inspire a gunner with confidence. These boxes, or batteries, were constructed on the principle of Ericson's *Monitor*—to show as little above the water as possible. A sinkbox was little more than a broad platform, ten feet long by six feet wide, with a coffin-shaped box "inletted" (sunken) into the center until it was flush around the deck. A canvas-covered framework was then attached to the edge of the platform to minimize the wash of the waves over the floating sculpture.

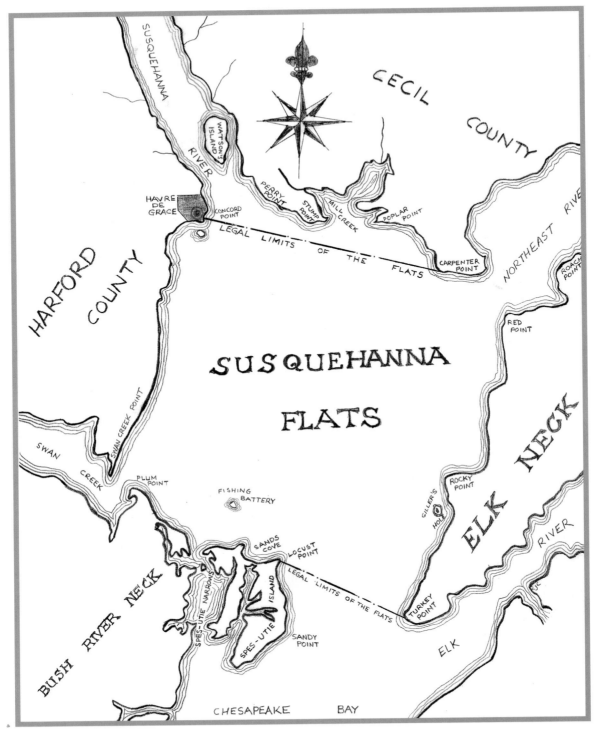

SUSQUEHANNA

FLATS

CECIL COUNTY

HARFORD COUNTY

SUSQUEHANNA RIVER

WATSON'S ISLAND

HAVRE DE GRACE

CONCORD POINT

PERRY POINT

STUMP POINT

MILL CREEK

POPLAR POINT

CARPENTER POINT

LEGAL LIMITS OF THE FLATS

NORTHEAST RIVER

ROACH POINT

RED POINT

ELK NECK

SWAN CREEK POINT

SWAN CREEK

PLUM POINT

FISHING BATTERY

ROCKY POINT

GILLER'S HOLE

ELK RIVER

SANDS COVE

LOCUST POINT

LEGAL LIMITS OF THE FLATS

BUSH RIVER NECK

SPES-UTIE NARROWS

SPES-UTIE ISLAND

SANDY POINT

TURKEY POINT

ELK

CHESAPEAKE BAY

Drawn by Roger J. Colburn, 1983

The stern of the *Reckless*. She was built in Havre de Grace in 1880 and registered as yacht license No. 8 issued by the Port of Baltimore. She had one mast, and her length was 62 feet 10 inches. Her net tonnage was 29.69. She was a sloop yacht with a plain head and a square stern.

The sinkbox was transported to the fowling grounds on a scow. One scow, "built and equipped after the most approved manner, especially to kill ducks in the Susquehanna and the upper bay" by Mr. J. W. McCullough of Port Deposit, is described by Krider:

> [The scow was] wall sided and flat-bottomed, forty feet long and nine feet beam. She carried a jib and a large fore and aft mainsail. A space barely sufficient for a tall man to lie at length, was decked off forward, and contained three or four bunks and a small stove, besides the stooling guns, several bags of heavy shot and kegs of ducking powder, not to speak of a quart coffee-pot and two large baskets of provender. This was the hardy duck-shooter's cabin; it was well pitched so as to be watertight, and was entered by a small scuttle with a slide; here he cooked, ate, slept, kept tally of his game, manufactured the heads and necks of decoys, cut his gun-wads, spun his yarns, drank his grog or coffee, and kept care outside from October until April, during the severest season of the year. . . . piled up in great heaps abaft [towards the stern] on either side, but so as not to interfere with the motions of the rudder, were the decoys or wooden ducks, each having its cord, with the weight attached, wound round its body, the last turn being taken round the neck, regular duck-shooter fashion. . . . The scow was furnished with raft-poles, and heavy oars or sweeps to be used in forcing her over the flats in a calm.

The sinkbox, or battery, itself rested midship.

The sinkbox was quite simply an appliance that allowed the gunner to hide below the surface of the water, preventing the ducks from seeing him until the proper moment. An early description of the operation of the sinkbox appeared in J. P. Giraud's *The Birds of Long Island* in 1844:

The gunner, by lying in the box on his back, is perfectly concealed, and having a large number of decoys around the battery, the deception is so perfect, that the birds often approach so near, as to give him an opportunity of discharging with effect two double barreled guns into a flock. Great havoc is made in this way, particularly among young birds. This mode of shooting requires two persons—one to shoot from the battery, the other to attend with a boat, to collect the dead birds, and drive up flocks sitting on the bay.

For comfort's sake, the bed of the box was prepared with hay or straw in the bottom, on which the shooter would lie. Oftentimes, a strap was fastened across the top of the gunner's feet to help him in rising. Because the mobility of the shooter was limited by his position in the box, his assistant would arrange the decoys, arraying them in such fashion that the ducks would be attracted in the direction most favorable to the shooter. The addition of a second gun often added considerably to the gunner's bag. On calm days, it was sometimes necessary for the gunner to raise his hands above the side of the box and imitate the motion of a duck flapping his wings, as if alighting on the water.

The sinkbox was designed for one purpose—to assist hunters in killing ducks—and its success was unprecedented; it was so successful that an article in a Baltimore newspaper from November 12, 1880, reported, "It is estimated in Havre de Grace by parties who handle ducks for the New York market, [that] 10,000 ducks were shot on the first Monday of November."

Nowhere was the sinkbox more widely used than on the Susquehanna Flats. The demands of the sinkbox shooters on "The Flats" created the need for thousands of duck decoys. Decoys from this region typically have well-rounded bottoms, regardless of whether they were made on the Harford or Cecil County side of the Susquehanna. The rarest of these sinkbox decoys were the flat-bottomed models used on the box itself. Those that were situated closest to the gunner were made of cast iron; their weight helped to submerge the device to a level even with the water line. Flat-bottomed wooden "wing ducks" were spread on the canvas wings of the box for additional camouflage. The basic design for the wing ducks was spelled out by Elisha J. Lewis in *The American Sportsman:* "the bodies of these ducks are reduced in bulk, or in other words, are shaved down to one-third their original thickness." Before the use of the cast-iron decoys and the wooden wing ducks, the profile of sinkboxes had been adjusted in the water by the use of stones laid upon the wings. The boxes would then be further disguised by covering the wings with sand and scattered sea-leaves, thereby creating the appearance of a sandbar.

Most of the major decoy makers of this era had iron flat-bottomed decoys cast from their own patterns. For the Upper Bay decoy makers, having the Whitaker Ironworks nearby at Principio Furnace in Cecil County proved to be a convenience. One member of the Whitaker family cast his iron decoys from his own pattern, which incorporated his raised initials "N.P.W." Iron decoys were sold by the pound. The ledger of James T. Holly of Havre de Grace, dated 1886, records that Holly sold 100 iron decoys, weighing 24 pounds each, to Commodore Richards from Oakington at 7¢ per pound, or $168.00 for the entire order.

Upper Bay decoy makers who produced birds for use on or around the sinkbox include John Holly and his son, James T. Holly, Benjamin Dye, John B. Graham, N. P. Whitaker, Leonard Pryor, Charles T. Wilson, James Currier, and Samuel T. Barnes. The Holly style of iron birds, both by John "Daddy" Holly and James T. Holly, are the standard most associated with sinkbox decoys. Unknown carvers, whose decoys are of equal importance to the area history, produced many others.

The popularity of sinkbox shooting on the Susquehanna Flats was widely known. An 1882 advertisement in the New York–based journal *Forest and Stream* offered for sale a handsome farm in Cecil County, Maryland, containing 115 acres. The farm, fronting on the Bohemia River near its junction with the Elk River, was listed with all furniture, stock, and produce to any "gentleman or club desiring a handsome shooting box or sinkbox and all necessary decoys."

During their heyday, about fifty sinkbox rigs operated out of Havre de Grace on the Flats. In 1891, deputy clerk of the Circuit Court of Harford County, William S. Forwood, traveled from Bel Air to Havre de Grace and issued a total of twenty-six licenses. In the *Aegis and Intelligencer* of November 6, a list of the sinkbox licensees was published: "John Poplar, Benjamin Kean, George R. Carver, E. F. Mitchell, P. M. Spencer, J. W. Chamberlain, E. G. Dern, W. H. Poplar, Leitheiser and Dobson, Wm. H. Myers, Wm. Dye, W. F. Day, John Keene, H. J. Poplar, E. E. Chesney, John McIl-

A steam yacht headed into Havre de Grace. The Concord Point lighthouse is in view at the left of the photograph.

A double stool on the Susquehanna Flats, 1923

heny, E. Madison Mitchell, Lewis Rickett (2), George W. Mitchell, Wm. E. Moore, Thomas Reynolds, S. T. Barnes, and George McCall, G. W. Barnes, Matthew Reynolds." In 1894, a sinkbox license cost $50 and a sneak boat license $20. The sinkbox license was assigned to the boat that transported the sinkboxes, rather than to the hunter, allowing one license to cover several sinkboxes operating out of the same scow. By that time, shooting was allowed only on Monday, Wednesday, and Friday. The state and county laws, regulating the best hunting grounds on the Chesapeake and its tributaries, became so stringent over time that duck shooting passed almost exclusively into the hands of two classes of hunters—professional gunners (market hunters) and wealthy sportsmen from Philadelphia, New York, and New England. In the log of Henry Keen and Joel Pusey, professional gunners from Havre de Grace, a good day of sinkboxing was recorded on November 19, 1926: 712 canvasbacks killed in a double stool (a pair of sinkboxes) off the Commodore's (Oakington).

Ferdinand C. Latrobe wrote in the *Maryland Conservationist:* "The sinkbox is in reality a floating blind. It is nothing more than an anchored box or coffin with hinged flaps to keep the water from invading it. It is a wholesale murdering sort of thing and has little 'sport' about it." In its report of the opening of the gunning season, the November 6, 1891, *Aegis and Intelligencer* observed, "On the Flats, sinkboxes secured from 30 to 100 to a box. . . . The decrease in the number of ducks can be appreciated from the fact that on the opening day in 1884 Mr. Wm. H. Dobson [of Havre de Grace] killed from a box 520 ducks."

The average good shot who was accustomed to shooting from a box could kill more birds than a comparable shot in a blind or pass shooting from a sandbar. The Susquehanna Flats were particularly favorable for sinkbox shooting because tens of thousands of ducks congregated there to feed on the lush beds of wild celery. The shooter had the best possible camouflage, and the birds were able to be shot at closer range. The wild celery grass also made the ducks harvested on the Upper Chesapeake highly desirable. The *Aegis and Intelligencer* of February 23, 1872, observed, "The canvas back duck of the Chesapeake is considered the best in the world, on account of the delicious flavor imparted to its flesh by the wild celery on which it feeds."

The exceptional effectiveness of the sinkbox and the increasing awareness of early conservationists led to increasingly stringent waterfowling regulations. But a proclamation issued by President Franklin D. Roosevelt on July 30, 1935, imposed the final blow to sinkbox shooting. Based upon recommendations of the U.S. Biological Survey and the secretary of the Department of Agriculture relative to the taking of migratory birds, the sinkbox was outlawed.

The elimination of the sinkbox caused quite a turmoil among the gunners who employed the device, for two reasons: no longer could they secure a stationary blind, and the sinkbox was simply the most successful of all means of waterfowling. Hunters from Harford, Cecil, and Kent Counties congregated on December 6, 1935, to protest the new regulations at a meeting called by Cecil County state senator Harold E. Coburn. Articles protesting the ban appeared in the local newspapers. The Baltimore *Sun* ran an article entitled "Gloom on the Susquehanna Flats." The *Havre de Grace Republican* published a story with this doomsday headline: "Only a few gunners try their luck for ducks on the opening day of the 1935–36 season." The State Game Division reported an estimated quarter million ducks in the vicinity of the Flats on that opening day. The outcry had no impact on the regulation. In Joel Pusey's journal of 1935, his last entry for the year expressed his feelings: "By order of J.N. Darling of the U.S. Biological Commission—sinkbox & bushwhack rigs are prohibited on Susquehanna Flats for the season of 1935. Such is life."

Since sinkbox decoys were no longer needed after the 1934–35 hunting season, and they were made from cast iron, their survival rate should have been quite good. But scrap iron in the mid-1930s had little value. If finished iron decoys were worth only seven cents per pound, what was their value to the gunner who no longer needed them for their intended purpose? Many became net anchors, and an equal number were likely discarded overboard. A pair of Charles T. Wilson cast-iron teal purchased from Madison Mitchell in the early 1970s had been presented to Mitchell by Edward Gather when he closed his scrap iron plant in Havre de Grace in 1958. Obviously many iron decoys went into the scrap furnace. The wooden wing ducks held their value to a hunter if they could be converted to floaters. In some cases, the attachment of a wooden keel gave them a second life. Others were converted by the addition of a bottom board. However, the time involved for the conversion of these decoys was hardly worth the effort, and many became firewood.

To claim that a gunning device is unique to a particular region invites controversy, yet the mention of the sinkbox immediately summons images of the Susquehanna Flats. The sinkbox was used up and down the Chesapeake, but it is with the Susquehanna Flats that it is most closely associated. In reference materials of the era, Havre de Grace, the sinkbox, canvasbacks, and decoys are closely related. Canvasbacks attracted the guns and gunners to the Susquehanna Flats, and the fate of the birds lay in the shadow of the deadly sinkbox. While history has duly recorded this way of life, the only tangible remnants of the days when "canvasback was king" and sinkboxes roamed the Flats are the cast-iron ducks and flat-bottomed wooden wing ducks.

Chesapeake Bay Retrievers

ROWING UP in Harford County in the 1950s afforded a young boy certain advantages. One among many was the ability to travel about freely without the worries of today. Even so, I was fortunate to have a constant security guard by my side. Monty, my ever-present companion, was a large, curly-coated, dark brown Chesapeake Bay retriever. He had been the family dog for a few years before my arrival, in Fallston in 1945. All of my parents' friends had Chesapeakes, or at least it seemed that way to me. If they had another breed of dog, it was some yappy little thing that in my young mind did not count as a serious dog. Monty had an odor about him that was totally unique, and when he got wet it was stronger. My father always said that this was his natural smell and that it was the lanolin in his coat, which would keep his skin dry when retrieving waterfowl. About the only thing that Monty ever retrieved was the occasional ball or stick. He escorted my grandfather to the Maryland and Pennsylvania Railroad station in Fallston and then returned home alone after Pop had safely boarded the train. Monty was ever faithful and very protective of my sister and me. There were certain visitors to our home whom Monty disliked from the start; perhaps they gave off an "I'm afraid of Monty" scent.

The day came in 1955 when Monty could no longer walk to and from the station. Sometimes he would manage the outbound half, but my father would have to take my green "Express" wagon and transport him home. My sister and I could not understand. Dad explained that Monty was old and that Chesapeakes have problems with arthritis in their old age. I find it easy to relate to those problems today. When Monty left us for good, he was buried near my grandfather's garden, where he would always be near Pop. Nicky and Amos followed Monty. They all looked and smelled the same, and each was protective and faithful to the end. A variety of other breeds lived with us over the years, but I still yearned for yet another Chessie. Then on July 11, 2001, in Brimfield, Massachusetts, at one of the largest outdoor antique shows in the country, I found him. My good friend Robert Hockaday and I were searching for the perfect antique, the best decoy, or the best artifact; we entered one of the "fields" at 11:45 anxiously awaiting the peal of the bell signaling the chaos which breaks loose precisely at noon. We split up—Bob went one way, I another.

I had traveled maybe fifty feet, watching while the huge crowds pushed and shoved to get a better look as the "stuff" came out of the station wagons, vans, and trucks, when I heard Bob yell, "Hey Buddy, get over here. Here it is! It's your dog!" There it was, a massive cast-iron dog right out of Baltimore or maybe New York. He looked just like a Hayward, Bartlett and Company Newfoundland dog, the progenitor of the powerful Chesapeake Bay retriever. He was lying down, massive legs and paws outstretched in front of him, his head erect, looking right at me. The dealing lasted all of about two minutes and it was done; he was my dog. He now rests on top of a blanket chest as the centerpiece of my living room.

Cast-iron garden statues were popular throughout America during the Victorian period. In the late 1850s the Baltimore Iron Works of Hayward, Bartlett and Company produced a variety of decorative iron items in addition to their stoves, archways, heating systems, structural pieces and architectural building fronts. They produced iron replicas of the first Newfoundland retrievers in America, Sailor and Canton, and placed one in front of their office on Light Street. When their office moved to Scott and Pratt Streets, the dog joined its mate to guard the front entrance. Hayward and Bartlett pursued their favorite recreation, waterfowling, with the same devotion and dedication with which they pursued their iron business. They gunned for ducks in Harford and Baltimore counties over decoys that wore cast-iron pads on their undersides as ballast weights with the raised initials of Thomas J. Hayward and Edward L. Bartlett. The cast-iron weights were manufactured at their foundry. These are the only weights of this style known in the decoy community.

The history of the Chesapeake Bay retriever is unique among dogs in America. According to the *Forest and Stream* magazine of December 1918, only two breeds of canine were, at that time, entitled to be called American—the Chesapeake Bay retriever and the Boston bull terrier. The breed descends directly from the Newfoundland retriever. Many stories have been told regarding the evolution of these dogs, including one claiming that Newfoundlands were crossed with sea otters. But the earliest and most accurate story was set forth in the following letter found in *The Dog and The Sportsman,* written by J. S. Skinner in 1845:

Baltimore, Maryland, January 7th 1845
My dear sir,—In the fall of 1807 I was on board of the ship Canton, belonging to my uncle, the late Hugh Thompson, of Baltimore, when we fell in, at sea, near the termination of a very heavy equinoctial gale, with an English brig in a sinking condition, and took off the crew. The brig was loaded with cod-fish, and was bound to Poole, in England, from Newfoundland. I boarded her, in command of a boat from the Canton, which was sent to take off the English crew, the brig's own boats having been all swept away, and her crew in a state of intoxication. I found on board of her two Newfoundland pups, male and female, which I saved, and subsequently, on our landing the English crew at Norfolk, our own destination being Baltimore, I purchased these two pups of the English captain for a guinea apiece. Being bound again to sea, I gave the dog pup, which was called *Sailor,* to Mr. John Mercer, of West River; and the slut

Seven young Chesapeakes at Marshy Point in 1929

THE NEWFOUNDLAND DOG. Original Breed.

The Newfoundland dog, original breed, as illustrated by J. S. Skinner, 1845

pup, which was called *Canton,* to Doctor James Stewart, of Sparrow's Point. The history which the English captain gave me of these pups was, that the owner of his brig was extensively engaged in the Newfoundland trade, and had directed his correspondent to select and send him a pair of pups of the most approved Newfoundland breed, but of different families, and that the pair I purchased of him were selected under this order. The dog was of a dingy red colour; and the slut black. They were not large; their hair was short, but very thick-coated; they had dew claws. Both attained great reputation as waterdogs. They were most sagacious in every thing; particularly so in all duties connected with *duck-shooting.* Governor Lloyd exchanged a merino ram for the dog, at the time of the merino fever, when such rams were selling for many hundred dollars, and took him over to his estate on the eastern shore of Maryland, where his progeny were well known for many years after; and may still be known there, and on the western shore, as the *Sailor breed.* The slut remained at Sparrow's Point till her death, and her progeny were and are still well known, through Patapsco Neck, on the Gunpowder, and up the bay, amongst the duck-shooters, as unsurpassed for their purposes. I have heard both Doctor Stewart and Mr. Mercer relate most extraordinary instances of the sagacity and performance of both dog and slut, and would refer you to their friends for such particulars as I am unable, at this distance of time, to recollect with sufficient accuracy to repeat.

'Yours, in haste, George Law'

Skinner then describes Sailor in the words of the dog's owner, Mr. Mercer:

On inquiry since the date of the above, of Mr. Mercer and of Dr. J. Stewart, it is ascertained of the former, who owned *Sailor,* that "he was of fine size and figure—lofty in his carriage, and built for strength and activity; remarkably muscular and broad across the hips and breast; head large, but not out of proportion; muzzle rather longer than is common with that race of dogs; his colour a dingy red with some white on the face and breast; his coat short *and smooth, but uncommonly thick,* and more like a coarse *fur* than hair; tail full, with long hairs, and always carried high. His eyes were very peculiar; they were so *light* as to have almost an unnatural appearance, something resembling what is termed a *wall* eye, in a horse; and it is remarkable, that in a visit which I made to the Eastern Shore, nearly twenty years after he was sent there, in a sloop which had been sent expressly for him, to West River, by Governor Lloyd, I saw many of his descendents who were marked with this peculiarity."

Harry Weiskittel with one of his Chesapeakes

As early as 1857, in *The Sportsman's Vade Mecum,* by "Dinks," the Chesapeake Bay retriever was recognized to be a "cross breed dog" and one of which there was "no true type." General Ferdinand C. Latrobe, who "ruled the kennels" at the Carroll's Island Ducking Club in Baltimore County, Maryland, in the nineteenth century, detailed the crosses that were to result in the Chesapeake Bay breed. His grandson, also named Ferdinand C. Latrobe, included this breeding history in his *Iron Men and Their Dogs.* According to General Latrobe, the breed began when progeny of the Newfoundlands were crossed with the local yellow and tan "coon dogs." Crosses with spaniels and "what-nots," or muts, about the countryside followed until the breed gained its distinctive liver color, strong power of scent, hardiness, shorter hair, medium size, and remarkable endurance. The love of water and the close, furry coat and excessive oil secretion that

Nellie bringing in a bluebill at Marshy Point 1938

make the dog able to withstand freezing temperatures in the water, as well as its general good temper, General Latrobe attributed to the Newfoundland. The water spaniel crosses, undoubtedly added from time to time, accounted for the superior retrieving qualities. The yellow and tan of hound, combined with the black and white of the Newfoundland and the varied-colored spaniel together produced the liver color so distinctive in the breed. Not satisfied with the "liver color," General Latrobe strove to establish a "sedge color" that would match the marsh grass wherein the dogs hide, to make them less easily seen by the wary waterfowl. The coloration of these dogs was also designated "Brown Winchester" or "Red Chester"; a dark reddish brown color on the back, which shaded lighter on the sides and became a very light yellow or white on the belly and inside of the legs. The throat and breast were often marked with white.

Unique to the Chesapeake Bay dog was its unusual coat. George L. Hopper describes it in his account of "Old Bob of Spesutia Island": "Old Bob . . . was a most perfect specimen of the rough or curly-coated dog. His outer coat was curled and twisted. . . . It felt to the hand like the wool of a Merino sheep; in color like the sands on the shore." This coat, as close, warm, and impervious as the skin of a seal, is found on no other dog, and it permits the Chesapeake to withstand the hardest weather and roughest water. It also gives the dog great advantage over the Newfoundland, who carries too much water in his long coat.

In *The American Kennel and Sporting Field* of 1882, Arnold Burges quoted the words of O. D. Foulks, a contributor to *The American Sportsman* from Cecil County, to describe the Chesapeake dog at work:

This breed of dogs are very swift and powerful swimmers, they will chase a crippled duck one and two miles, and unless the bird be very slightly hit, will catch him in the end. The dog sits on the shore behind the blind, his color matching so well with the sand and clay that were he even continually moving the ducks would never notice him. He seldom moves any part of his body except the head, which he continually turns up and down the river, often sighting the approaching duck before the gunner. When the gun is fired and a duck falls, he bounds to the edge of the water, plunges in and brings it ashore, and then without having received a word of command from his master, carries it up to the place where he sits and drops it. After giving himself two or three shakes and a roll, he resumes his old station and watch. He does not shiver like a setter, or raise and drop his fore-feet like a wet spaniel; the shaking he has given his coarse, oily coat, has freed it entirely from the ice and water. If one of the fallen birds chance to be only crippled, he swims past the dead ones, keeping the wounded duck in sight; when it dives he swims to the spot and there continues turning round and round, now and then throwing himself high in the water, especially if the waves are heavy. As soon as the duck reappears, he strikes out immediately for it, and as it dives again he swims to the spot where he last saw it, and continues to turn until the duck comes up, then another swim, and so on until the duck is tired out.

The Chesapeakes were well known for their ability to sense flocks of ducks at great distances. They would indicate to their masters by their behavior the approach of flocks that were too distant for the human eye to notice. They would remain frozen in place until shots were fired, then mark the location of the fallen fowl prior to jumping to retrieve. The usual method of retrieval by the Chesapeakes was one duck at a time, but occasionally multiple ducks would be brought back. In 1898, Thomas Cadwalader, in the Maxwell's Point journal, mentioned a dog with memorable retrieving qualities: "Mr. Dryer came from his house up the river at dead of night in a small horse-trough which could not be paddled back if there was any wind, ergo he spent some time here. He brought a fierce Chesapeake called 'Rose' which retrieved come il faut. He threatened to present us with her son which he did later."

The Civil War had an adverse impact on Chesapeake Bay retrievers, according to Foulks. While once everyone living on a ducking shore owned one two of the breed, the war scattered families; and "newcomers" to the region either did not know the value of the breed or did not take interest in anything outside the farm, neglecting good breeding of the dogs. In spite of the apparent decline in the numbers of Chesapeakes after the Civil War, the breed persevered and was well recognized by 1877, when Chesapeake Bay Ducking Dogs appeared as a class at the Poultry and Fanciers Association Show, held at the Maryland Institute in Baltimore. A report in the *Aegis and Intelligencer* of January 5th of that year, under the heading "Harford at the Dog Show," mentioned that a prize was given for the best couple of Chesapeake Bay Ducking Dogs. The next week's edition of that same newspaper reported, "Mr. S. N. Hyde's ducking dog Jim attracted marked attention from sportsmen during the exhibition." A com-

The Weiskittel Christmas card, showing Sammy Green bringing one in

mittee of sportsmen was formed at the 1877 show with the express purpose of establishing standards and classes for the breed, and at a subsequent meeting, the committee's report divided the breed into three classes, "the Otter dog, a tawny sedge color with wavy brown hair, the Curly Dog, and the Straight-haired dog, both of a red-brown color," and set 80 pounds as the minimum weight of a two-year-old (Latrobe's *Iron Men and Their Dogs*). A few years later, when the Chesapeake Bay Dog Club came into being, the standards were narrowed yet further.

The Chesapeake Bay Dog Club was established on April 17, 1890, with Edward L. Bartlett as president. The objects of the club were set forth in their constitution and by-laws:

> The object of the Club shall be to promote the breeding of Chesapeake Bay Dogs; to develop and bring to perfection their natural high qualities for retrieving fowl and ability to stand severe exertion and strain during the most severe winter weather; to define and publish a description of their true type; to urge the adoption of such type upon breeders, competitors at ducking points and

Edward Wright on the pier at Marshy Point with two Chesapeakes and a pile of decoys

C. John Sullivan, Jr., and Susan Blair Sullivan
with ever-faithful Monty

Stockton, Maryland, November 1910, a young
hunter with his dog and game

bench shows and others as the standard by which Chesapeakes should be judged; to encourage competition of this breed at such places, and to suggest to all associations and shows where Chesapeakes compete, the names of qualified and proper judges.

On the same day, the club adopted the standard of the breed. The "value of points" was established as follows: head, including ears, lips, and eyes, 14; neck, 6; shoulders and chest, 14; back, quarters, and stifles, 14; legs, elbows, hocks, and feet, 14; stern, 4; symmetry and quality, 6; coat and texture, 16; color, 12. A committee described the standard in detail:

CHESAPEAKE BAY DOG

Descriptive List

Head: Broad, running to nose, only a trifle pointed, but not at all sharp. Eyes of yellow color. Ears small, placed well up on head. Face covered with very short hair.

Neck: Should be only moderately long and with a firm, strong appearance.

Shoulders and Chest: Should have full liberty with plenty of show for power and no tendency to restriction of movement. Chest strong and deep.

Back Quarters & Stifles: Should show fully as much, if not more, power than fore quarters and be capable of standing prolonged strain. Any tendency to weakness must be avoided. Ducking on the broad waters of the Chesapeake Bay involves at times facing a heavy tide and sea, and in cases of following wounded fowl a dog is frequently subjected to a long swim.

Legs, Elbows, Hocks & Feet: Legs should be short, showing both bone and muscle and with well webbed feet of good size; fore legs rather straight and symmetrical. It is to be understood that short legs does not convey the idea of a dumpy foundation. Elbows well let down and set straight for development of easy movement.

Stern: Should be stout, somewhat long, the straighter the better, and showing only moderate feather.

Symmetry and Quality: The Chesapeake Bay Dog should show a bright, lively, intelligent expression, with general outline good at all points; in fact a dog worthy of notice in any company.

Coat and Texture: Short and thick, somewhat coarse, with tendency to wave over shoulders, back and loins, where it is longest; nowhere over one and a quarter to one and a half inches long. That on flanks, legs and belly shorter, tapering to quite short near the feet. Under all this a short, woolly fur, which should well cover the skin and can be observed by pressing aside the outer coat. This coat preserves the dog from the effect of wet and cold and enables him to stand severe exposure; a shake or two throwing off all water, and is conducive to speed in swimming.

Color: Nearly resembling wet sedge grass, though towards Spring it becomes lighter by exposure to weather. A small white spot or frill on breast is admissible. Color is important, as the dog in most cases is apt to be outside the blind, consequently too dark is objectionable; the deep liver of the Spaniel making much greater contrast therefore is to be avoided.

Weight: Should be about sixty-five (65) pounds, too large a dog being unwieldy and lacking quickness of movement. Bitches usually smaller than the dog, but not necessarily so.

This Scale and Descriptive List is the Standard for judging Chesapeake Bay Dogs as agreed upon by the Committee appointed by the American Kennel Club, and forwarded to Secretary, American Kennel Club September 26th, 1885.

James F. Pearson,
Isaac T. Norris,
H. Malcolm
Committee

The pride of ownership and the competition among dog owners for what they considered best of breed were apparent among the various gunning clubs. Henry Thomas Weld, the president of the San Domingo Gunning Club, in 1891, wrote, "I think that we have now the most unexceptionable kennel of Chesapeake Bay dogs in the State and I have promised Lynch to send him a puppy from the next litter of that ever beautiful and well bred dog Keziah—I think that without any exception she is the handsomest animal I have ever seen—and as kind and gentle as possible." The gunning clubs employed experienced gunners, who understood the habits and nature of wildfowl. The gunners assisted with the placing of decoys and managed the boats and the kennels. One of these men, Mr. John Sweeting, occupied such a position at Mr. Weld's club. This position would be comparable to the master of hounds at a foxhunting club. In addition to being perfectly familiar with the habits and movement of wildfowl, Sweeting was considered to be one of the finest shots on Chesapeake waters. A writer in the *Baltimore County Union* of April 10, 1886, stated, "[Mr. John Sweeting] has but one peer to my knowledge—that is, Mr. Edward Lynch, who occupies a similar position with the Maxwell's Point Club. The two combined form a team unequaled as marksmen on wing or rapid flight shooting. They also keep ten or twelve pure-bred Chesapeake Bay dogs. These dogs are remarkable for wonderful sagacity and great powers of endurance in retrieving game amid icy waters. The sagacity of some of that breed nearly rises to the level of reason." For his valued service, Edward Lynch received a salary of $40 per month in 1891.

The value placed on Chesapeake Bay retrievers by their owners can be seen in this ad from the Baltimore *Sun* of December 17, 1859: "Strayed— From No. 37 Mulberry street, a well-grown liver-colored Newfoundland DOG, with a few spots on his front paws. Answers to the name of Jack. A reward of three dollars ($3) will be given for his return." In the same issue, a mere $5 is offered for the return of the *Seagull,* a 30-foot sailboat that had been stolen. In 1916, the price to purchase a good, trained Chesapeake exceeded $100. An ad entitled "Chesapeake Bay Duck Retrievers" placed by the Chesapeake Kennel of Lee Hall, Virginia, in the November issue of *Outing* read: "A pair of thoroughly broken Chesapeake Bay Duck Retrievers (dogs) Pedigreed and Registered. Trained and used by a market gunner. Broken to boat, marsh and blind shooting. Few dogs their equal as Duck retrievers. Price $150.00 each."

The Chesapeake Bay dog experienced increasing popularity in succeeding years, when duck gunning was at its peak on Maryland shores; this popularity spread even into the Midwest and Far West states. By 1932, however, many debated the talents of the "Chessie" versus the Labrador and the Irish spaniel. Freeman Lloyd, writing for the *Sportsman,* quoted Charles W. Berg, a Chesapeake breeder and experienced duck hunter, who gave credit to the Irish spaniel as the fastest retriever and to the Labrador as the easiest to break. But Berg summarized the "unexplainable" superiority of the Chesapeake when he wrote:

> He can experience more hardship than any individual dog on earth and go on doing his work just as though obstacles were not in his path. The right kind of Chesapeake Bay dog will stay on game and bring it back to you if he has to travel five miles to get his bird. And he won't come back without it. He will go through ice, swift current, and freezing water; in bogs and marshes up to his neck; and come back with the pride and expression of a scientist who has made a contribution to humanity. I have seen them work in cold salt water, from sunup to sundown and never refuse to retrieve. Water so cold that a human being

could not hold his hand in it for two minutes and never refuse to retrieve. I have had dark sedge-colored Chesapeake Bay dogs many, many times retrieve ducks for me when they were frozen so solid with ice that when they came back on the marsh you could hear the ice crackle on their bodies.

As William C. Hazelton so aptly put it in a 1928 issue of the *Maryland Conservationist,* "To them life begins and ends tolling and retrieving ducks."

The Chesapeake Bay breed continues to thrive to this day. Its remarkable instincts to retrieve, its natural ability to mark ducks before the hunter hears or sees them, its powerful endurance in working in the iciest waters, and its steadfast loyalty have contributed to the breed's success. The men that developed this unique breed of American canine were neither dog breeders nor retriever trainers. They depended on the breed's innate qualities, which served to establish its superiority as a retriever. Just as the duck decoy is a genuine and unique American art form, the Chesapeake Bay retriever is quintessentially American.

You who wander hither,
Pass not unheeded
This spot, where poor Sailor
Is deposited.
He was born of Newfoundland parents;
His vigilance during many years
Was the safeguard of Cedar Point.
His talents and manners were long
The amusement and delight
Of those who resorted to it.
Of his unshaken fidelity,
Of his cordial attachment
To his master and his family,
A just conception cannot
Be conveyed by language,
Or formed but by those
Who intimately knew him.

J. S. Skinner
The Dog and the Sportsman

Waterfowling Firearms

As LONG AS I can recall, the attic of my family's house held a fascination for me. It was the hiding place for treasures of days gone by—oil lamps, the Victrola, stacks of old records, long-forgotten trunks—seasonal decorations, and a well-hidden Christmas gift that surely had my name on it. All were neatly arranged, each having its very own space. My trips alone to the garret were quick ones; it was either too hot or too cold. The only perfect days were the semiannual rug changing days, but my father, grandfather, or an uncle was along for those trips. Finally, on one of those days when the winter rugs went up and the summer rugs came down, I lagged behind in the attic. It was the perfect opportunity to do some exploring. I climbed over some low boards, gaining access to the center dormer; the warm sun shining in the dormer window made the areas where the bark had peeled from the ancient chestnut timbers shine as if they were polished. I saw the base to a "Gone With the Wind" lamp, several gray crocks, and what appeared to be the barrel of an old gun. Just as I reached for the barrel, I heard the voices of my father and grandfather, who were coming up the steps with another rug. I feared that it was too late—I was caught somewhere where I shouldn't have been—I was surely in trouble. But my find was as much a treat for them as it was for me, and in short order they were helping me out of the dormer, bringing with them the gun barrel, the wooden stock, and the gun's fore end. I had just reintroduced those two generations to their old shotgun. The relic had been handed down to my grandfather and then to my father. At that point it became mine, and it has stayed with me to this day. It was nothing very fancy or fine, but to me it was a genuine artifact of my family's gunning heritage. I'm not sure if the gun had ever shot a rabbit or squirrel, but to the mind of that nine-year-old boy it had slaughtered more fowl than one could dream of. It took up residence on a rack on my bedroom wall; it traveled to elementary school with me for "show and tell" and on May Day when I played the role of Daniel Boone. My treasure was in fact a twelve-gauge, breech-loading, Damascus steel, Belgian-made shotgun with the words *The Interchangeable* inscribed on its side plates. A German silver inletted six-point star decorated the butt of the checkered pistol grip, and the initials CJS had been carved on the left side of the stock by my father when he was about my age. The star entitled me to some rank, I felt, as I pursued the "bad guys" that young boys are always attempting to free the world from, and the CJS personalized my gun and saved me the trouble of carving on the walnut stock myself. The old gun was loose from age, and the barrel would rattle against the receiver with the slightest jerk. The thought of putting a live shell in the barrel never crossed my mind. I found loading tools for shells in the smokehouse, along with cleaning rods and round, brass wire cleaning brushes; they were in their neat-looking original box, *The Ideal Gun Cleaner,* patented April 9, 1901. Years later, the original wooden gun box was uncovered at the opposite end of the attic. The discovery of that old gun, my most cherished gun, led me to search for others; that search holds the same fascination for me today that my own attic did decades ago.

The technical advancements in firearms from the settlement of North America through the 1930s were enormous. The early colonists were armed with flintlock muskets, the style which prevailed until the mid-1800s. By 1843, imported muzzle-loading fowling pieces were readily available in Maryland; W. H. and E. Soper, of 44 South Charles Street in Baltimore, advertised in the *Baltimore American* on August 29 of that year the availability of "350 Guns and Fowling Pieces, comprising a general assortment from the small bird to ducking gun, both single and double barrel. This sale will afford a good assortment for dealers in guns to purchase a supply." The *Baltimore Patriot* of November 22, 1845, featured in its classified ads "Duck Guns . . . Fowling Pieces . . . and Percussion CAPS" from Schaeffer and Loney and "Du Pont's Ducking Powder . . . manufactured for DUCK SHOOTING" for sale by Z. H. Cooch. Duck shooting was not the only sport of the day; an announcement of a "Foot Race" with a prize of $500 was also featured. It is a sign of the times in this border state with southern sympathies that, alongside the ads for ducking equipment, "A Young Negro Man for Sale for Life" was offered. In the *American and*

Clark and Sneider ran their advertisement for conversion of muzzle-loader to breech-loader on December 19, 1873.

(*Top*) Hollis and Company 4-gauge muzzle-loader, made in London, circa 1840, used at General George Cadwalader's Maxwell's Point; and (*bottom*) Clark and Sneider 10-gauge breech-loaded double barrel, serial number 21, made in Baltimore, Maryland

Commercial Advertiser of Baltimore of January 5, 1856, the Sportsman's Warehouse advertised: "I am now receiving per steamers and packets from Europe a large and well selected stock of SINGLE and DOUBLE GUNS, to which I would respectfully call the attention of the trade and all persons in want of fowling pieces." By 1858, there were sixteen gunsmiths listed in the *Business Directory of Baltimore City.*

The loading of early fowling pieces was a slow and tedious process. The barrel of the musket was loaded with powder, shot, and a felt wad (to hold the charge in place) at its muzzle end. A piece of flint was used to create a spark when the trigger was pulled. A tiny hole at the breech end of the barrel would permit the spark from the flint to ignite the powder, thus causing the powder to explode, propelling the shot out of the barrel. Precision in the measuring of the powder and shot was imperative, or the end result could be a deadly experience for the shooter or his companion. The size of the shot pellets and the quantity of shot and powder had to be adjusted depending upon the species of fowl to be hunted and the style of shooting that was to be employed. Achieving consistency in these "loads" was a constant challenge with these firearms.

Shot pellets of uniform size and high quality came into being around 1770. To produce the shot, molten lead was poured from a tower into a large tank of chilled water. Screen grids of varying sizes were used to form pellets of specific sizes. The *Baltimore Daily American,* in their annual statement of trade and commerce for Baltimore for the year 1860, reported that the consumption of pig lead by the Merchant Shot Tower Company of Baltimore City amounted to 400 tons. Of this, 350 tons was manufactured into shot, the equivalent of 28,000 bags of shot. Baltimore-made shot always enjoyed an excellent reputation, "in consequence," the *Daily American* report declared, "of their perfect sphericity and the superiority of their finish." Efforts were made in other cities, especially New York, to surpass Baltimore's product, but to no avail. "The excellence of the Baltimore-manufactured article secures it a preference wherever known."

One of the earliest technical advancements was a change from the flintlock to a percussion cap mechanism. By the 1850s, percussion muzzle-loaders were beginning to replace flintlocks. When the trigger was pulled, the cocked hammer struck a percussion cap, resting on a raised nipple, which created a spark. A tiny hole permitted the spark generated by the snapped cap to ignite the powder and create the explosion, which blasted the shot from the muzzle of the gun. These fowling pieces were available in a variety of gauges, or bores, ranging from a 2-bore to a 20-bore (the smaller the number the larger the diameter of the barrel). Gauge numbers are based on the number of round balls whose combined weight equals one pound. The diameter of each ball will match exactly the diameter of the gun barrel. A round ball, ten of them weighing a pound, will fit precisely in the barrel of a 10-gauge, eight balls weighing a pound will fit in an 8-gauge, and so forth for each gauge. All of these firearms were fired from the shoulder.

Alexander McComas and Son's advertisement as it appeared in the *Aegis and Intelligencer* of November 6, 1891

Technical advancements in shotguns: (*top*) Remington Arms Company 12-gauge automatic Model 11, patented 1900; (*center*) Winchester Model 1897 pump-action 12-gauge; (*bottom*) Winchester Model 1886 lever-action 12-gauge

Larger-bore guns were manufactured by both gunsmiths and blacksmiths and were used specifically for shooting ducks bedded in flocks upon the water. As early as 1832 their use was prohibited in certain Maryland waters. Some of these cannon measured 8 feet in length with an end-of-muzzle diameter of over 2 inches. The idea of these "punt guns" was to kill as many ducks as possible with one shot; they were used at night by market hunters, and rarely did the hunter have the opportunity of a second shot. These guns were fired from gunning skiffs, where they would rest on sandbags or be fastened to the skiff with iron trunnions mounted on each side of the breech. In addition to these punt guns, outlaw gunners designed muzzle-loading battery guns, which incorporated five to seven gun barrels into a single unit. These guns were created by inserting pipes into blocks of wood and attaching the muzzle-loading apparatus to ignite the powder.

The powers of invention advanced quickly during the Industrial Revolution, bringing about major changes in firearm technology. Breech-loading guns were quickly replacing muzzle-loaders. Paper cartridges were developed which held both powder and shot as well as the percussion cap necessary for ignition. These advancements promoted the goals of shooters spelled out in 1864 by "Marksman" (Frank Forester) in *The Dead Shot*: "The crowning feature in every gun is the force and effect with which it throws the shot: the gun which will throw the shot sharpest and strongest, and consequently killing the fartherest, is, to all intents and purposes, the better gun in the hands of a good sportsman." Public tests were held between breech-loaders and muzzle-loaders. Numerous guns of the same caliber by various makers were loaded with shot and powder charges of the same size and measure used by both sides and with targets placed at precisely the same distances. The conclusions reached determined that the breech-loaders would require an extra charge of powder for results equivalent to the muzzle-loaders. The results of these tests, which were made public through all the sporting papers of the time, showed that "undoubtedly, the most perfect and useful gun in the hands of a sportsman is that which possesses the power of shooting strongest and fartherest with the smallest charges." Nevertheless, these tests did not convince most gunners, and the popularity of the breech-loader increased.

Charles Edward Sneider, who worked as a gunsmith in Baltimore for the merchant Thomas P. Poultney, was granted his first patent on March 20, 1860, for a top latch, which allowed a shotgun to be opened at the breech (the barrel's end above the trigger). This made loading a much quicker and simpler operation than in the past.

Sneider formed a partnership with Duncan C. Clark and designed and manufactured breech-loading ducking guns on Sharpe Street in Baltimore. They advertised in newspapers that "altering" muzzle-loading guns to breech-loaders was their specialty. In the Clark and Sneider catalog of 1878, the announcement of their "highest centennial medal for workmanship" was featured, and their finest-grade shotgun was advertised for $300, while the price for conversion from muzzle-loader to breech-loader was $75. Testimonials published in the catalog complimented the firm's expertise. Mr. P. W. Lippitt of Hartford, Connecticut, wrote, "I most cheerfully say that the alteration of my Greener Exhibition Gun from a muzzle to a breech-loader is to my entire satisfaction, no one could say from the style and workmanship that it was ever any thing else but a breech-loader, I have shown it to a number of my friends, and they all pronounce it the best done job they had ever seen; I shall take pleasure in recommending your work." A testimonial by the famous decoy maker from the eastern shore of Virginia, Nathan F. Cobb, for a Clark and Sneider gun appeared in that same catalog.

Sneider is credited by some with the development of choke-boring, in which the end of the barrel at the muzzle has a smaller internal diameter than at the chamber or trigger end. This tapering of the barrel holds the shot in a tighter pattern. While this improvement is attributed to others, in the 1870s, some suggest that Sneider was using this innovation in Europe as early as 1846. By 1895, all choke-bored guns were tested for the pattern of shot at a 30-inch circle at a distance of 40 yards from the muzzle of the gun. The following percentages were established according to the bore of the muzzle: for a cylinder bore, 35–40 percent of the shot would hit within the circle; for a barrel with a light choke, 40–52 percent; medium choke, 50–60 percent; "full" choke, 58–65 percent; and an "extra full" choke, 60–67 percent.

In competition with the Clark and Sneider firm was Alexander McComas, in business since 1843 and located at 51 South Calvert Street. McComas advertised "Sporting Apparatus, Ammunition, and material for gunmakers etc. wholesale and retail. Guns made to order and repaired in the best manner." McComas advertised in the small towns as well. In the *National American,* published in Bel Air, on September 18, 1857, McComas announced that he "weekly receives additions to his already large assortment of double and single DUCK AND BIRD GUNS." Out-of-state gun dealers recognized the market that existed for their products beyond the big cities and near the fowling grounds; John Krider, of Second and Walnut Streets in Philadelphia, advertised his shotguns and his new book, *Krider's Sporting Anecdotes,* in the August 16, 1855, edition of the *Harford Madisonian and Havre de Grace Advertiser.* Not all gunners could afford to purchase their equipment, so some rented it. Wertsner and Morris, of 2 Light Street, advertised "guns, ammunition, rifles, revolvers, and guns for hire by day or week" in the program of the Fifth Annual Fair of the Cecil County Agricultural Society of 1886. Other gunners purchased used guns for reasonable prices: the account book of C. C. Pusey's store reports that on December 17, 1878, a "used fowling piece" was ordered from Baltimore for Bob Holloway for $5. Imported guns continued to challenge the American ingenuity. The gun manufacturer W. W. Greener, of Birmingham and London, England, advertised his "Far-Killing Duck Gun" in the *Forest and Stream* magazine of March 30, 1880: "These guns unlike American machine made arms, have Straight Barrels, Safe Locks, and every limb in due proportion to the caliber and weight of the Gun, and all bear the Government Proof Marks."

Soon to follow was the development of cartridges that held accurately measured loads of powder and shot. By the late 1800s, Montgomery Ward and Company was selling its "Nitro Powder Blue Label" shells, handloaded by professional trap shots on their premises, for $2.00 per hundred.

In 1887, the Winchester Arms Company introduced the first repeating lever action shotgun and the first pump action shotgun. Both of these guns were capable of firing multiple shots by either a cock of the lever or a pump of the fore end. The lever action would cock the gun and eject the

In February 1912 this gunner shot 3 geese with his 10-gauge lever-action
Winchester Model 1887.

spent shell with a single stroke of the lever. The pump action accomplished the same task with a continuous motion of sliding the fore end forward then back for each shot fired. An ad in the *Sports Afield* magazine of April 1894 illustrates the deadly speed of these guns in its description of a 12-gauge repeating shotgun manufactured by the Burgess Gun Company, Buffalo, New York: "Latest, Quickest, Simplest, Safest. The ideal action. Movement in direct line between points of support. Double hits in 1/8 second; three hits in one second; six hits in less than three seconds." In a matter of approximately 90 years the waterfowler had been able to increase his chances of shooting the migrant birds with one or two shots to several in approximately the same amount of time or less.

The final and perhaps the most deadly advance in shotgun production was the invention of the automatic shotgun. John Moses Browning had more impact on the production of firearms than perhaps any individual in history. With over 100 patents credited to him, he was to change the methods and style of waterfowling forever. In 1899 John Browning presented his design for an auto-loading shotgun to the Winchester Arms Company. Winchester was content to manufacture the lever action and pump action shotguns (also of Browning's design) and postponed consideration of the auto-loader. Browning then approached Remington Arms, but the untimely death of Remington's president sent Browning off on his own. He ordered his newly patented gun from Fabrique Nationale in Belgium. The first 10,000 guns arrived in the United States in 1904. The auto-loader was to be known as the Browning Auto-5. Once these guns were loaded, all that was necessary for the gunner to do was to pull the trigger. The gases produced by the fired shell not only ejected the spent cartridge but loaded the next round into the chamber. Factories and gunsmiths alike provided extended ammunition tubes for these new auto-loaders. These tubes extended the magazines, making the gun capable of holding up to ten cartridges. The combination of a well-placed blind, a bushwhack boat or sinkbox, and a gunner equipped with one of these guns was more devastating to the migrating fowl than anyone could have conceived of just a few years before. The biennial "Statement of the Permanent Wild Life Protection Fund" published in 1915 remarked on these guns as follows:

> The makers of state laws are very much to blame for the increasing circulation and use of these reprehensible machines for slaughter.
>
> There now lies before me an advertisement of an "extension" for the magazines of automatic shotguns, increasing by four the number of cartridges that can be fired without removing the gun from the shoulder. In other words, with the "extension" (costing only $5), ten shots now can be fired by ten pulls of the trigger without once stopping to reload the gun!
>
> Undoubtedly, the owners of automatic and pump guns would use Gatling guns on American game if they could. In many states, aye, even in New York, the desire among certain hunters for automatic guns amounts to a perfect craze. During the six months following its first appearance, the supply of the new Winchester Automatic was months behind the demand. These weapons seem to be specially desired by poor shots, in order to help out their daily showing, and make themselves seem more like real sportsmen; and no gunner is too poor to pay his $35 for one of these weapons. . . .
>
> The trouble with these machine guns lies in the fact that they increase the slaughter of wildfowl by enabling both good shots and poor shots to kill about fifty per cent more ducks and geese than the same men could kill with ordinary double-barreled guns, removed from the shoulder after every two shots. If this is not true then all the men who own the slaughter guns have been cajoled out of their money.
>
> The principles of the devotees of the rod are exactly the reverse of the lack of principles of the machine gunners. To increase the difficulties of angling and to give the game more of a show, the former have steadily reduced the size of their lines and weight of their rods. The automatic gunner wants the utmost of machinery, and every chance of escape taken away from the ducks and geese. But it is useless to comment on that. No gentleman sportsman now uses a machine gun, and the man who does use one does not know that there is any such thing as ethics in shotgun sport. They are in the class of "sports" who dynamite trout and kill robins for food.

While some hunters relied on the automatic weapons to increase their daily bags, other true sporting types rejected these new guns. An eighteen-year-old Robert C. Walker of Washington, D.C., who vacationed annually in Ocean City, Maryland, and who gunned there daily, obviously felt the auto-loading guns were not as sporting as the traditional double barrels. He wrote in his daily journal on December 23, 1912, "I traded my auto-loading gun with extra barrel and case in for $30 on the purchase of a Fox double barrel shotgun price $49.50 of Geo. A. Emmons successor to Wm. Wagner #16,769 Grade AE with automatic ejector. During season of 1912 I used about 895 shells, brought 33 home and had the balance of the thousand used by my father, the Dominican Brothers and my guests."

By 1930, the Remington Arms Company had made a significant change in the production of their auto-loading shotgun, which, since 1911, had relied on the patents of John M. Browning. These automatics, which had been designed to fire five to ten rounds, were now modified, reducing the capacity of the gun to three shells. They named this new shotgun "The Sportsman." It had been developed "to meet the demands of a great many hunters who feel that three shots, without reloading, are ample for all practical shooting requirements." The Izaak Walton League of America endorsed this gun at their annual American Game Conference, where they passed the following resolution: "We especially commend such steps as a recently announced Small-Bore Shotgun which cannot be fired more than three times without reloading."

The changes in firearm technology from the mid-1800s to the invention of the auto-loader in 1899 followed each other in rapid succession. These developments changed gunning styles and methods forever. The automatic shotgun was more devastating to the migratory fowl than the illegal large-bore firearms of prior decades. If one benefit to the fowl from firearm innovation could be cited, it would be the conservation laws of 1934–35 that resulted. This legislation was enacted to address the depletion of the migratory flocks brought about in part by the invention of the auto-loading shotgun.

For those who value the sport, hunting includes an array of elements, and the size of the take is not primary. My recollections of the hunt are much more than the number of birds killed. It is the experience of the day that is recalled. If a duck or goose is never seen, it is being in nature with good friends and sharing how cold it was, how hot it was, how wet we got, or the ones that got away that we speak of.

Grover Cleveland spoke for all waterfowlers when in 1903 he wrote "How True Duck Hunters Stand Together":

> When the ducks have ceased to fly for the day the serene duck hunter returns to camp in a tranquil, satisfied frame of mind befitting his fraternity membership. He has several ducks actually in hand, and he has fully enjoyed the self-deception and pretense which have led him to the belief that he has shot well. His few confessed misses are all satisfactorily accounted for; and he is too well broken to the vicissitudes of duck shooting, and too old a hunter, to be cast down by the

bad fortune which has thickly scattered, over distant water and marshes, his un-recovered dead.

When at the close of such a day a party of serene duck hunters are gathered together, a common fund of adventure is made up. Each as he contributes his share is entitled to add such embellishments of the imagination as will make his recital most interesting to his associates and gratifying to himself; and a law tac-itly adopted but universally recognized by the company binds them all to an unquestioning acceptance of the truth of every narration. The successes of the day as well as its incidence of hard luck, and every excuse and explanation in mitigation of small returns of game, as they are rehearsed, create lively interest and quiet enjoyment. The one thing that might be a discordant note would be a hint or confession of downright and inexcusably bad shooting.

It is always the stories that tie us to the sport. One such story of a day of sport on Maryland's Eastern Shore took place in 1975. I had purchased a Remington Model 11 auto-loading shotgun with an extended tube that had been used by a market hunter from Havre de Grace before the water-fowling regulations of the 1930s. Although the tube measured only 8 ¼ inches, it would hold far more shells than the law allowed. The sight of the tube alone would send chills down the spine of any God-fearing fowl. However, the tube had been plugged to hold the legally permitted three shells. That same year I had the opportunity to go goose hunting in Dor-chester County on the farm of state senator Frederick Malkus, with two Harford County dignitaries—W. Robert Wallis, the editor of the county newspaper, and William H. Cox, Jr., a member of the Maryland House of Delegates. The senator's farm lay adjacent to the Blackwater National Wildlife Refuge just outside of Cambridge. The morning was off to an in-teresting start when the gentleman from the Harford County delegation was admonished for loading his gun in the hunting lodge while it was still pitch black outside. "Unload that gun," the senator said, "You think there's a grizzly bear waiting outside the door for you?" The delegate meekly ejected the loaded shells and out the door we were led, me to a field pit, the others to a water blind. It was miserably cold, damp, and dark inside that buried metal dumpster. I was sitting on a plastic bucket, my feet resting in about three inches of icy water, and I had no idea where my gunning comrades were. About fifteen minutes before daylight, that won-derful sound of a thousand or more Canada geese woke my senses. Here they come; I knew they would. But in reality, they were leaving the sen-ator's fields and heading back to the refuge for the day. I was never sure if it was the wind from their wings or a change in my anticipation, but the morning seemed to grow colder as the sun rose over the marshes. Hours later, one lone goose appeared in the sky out of nowhere, directly in my sights. Was it an apparition or a big fat Canada goose? There he was, above me, the proper angle, the proper distance, the perfect shot. I raised that historic automatic shotgun, thinking of the thousands of birds it had dropped. Bang! Click. Nothing. The shell had jammed, with the spent shell lodged in the action. That "infallible" goose-killing machine was done for the day. The goose reached my partners just after the shot from my lone shell showered them like icy sleet. They raised their guns. Bang! Bang! Bang! The lone goose honked and headed back to the refuge, not a mark on him. My excuse—the auto-loader malfunctioned; their excuse—that I had tried to shoot them. It's always the stories we tell that keep us going back for more "sport."

> It was on this day that I once or twice had my "eye wiped," and I recall it even now with anything but satisfaction. It is a provoking thing to miss a fair shot, but to have your companion after you have had your chance knock down the bird by a long, hard shot makes one feel somewhat distressed. This we call "wiping the eye"; but I have always thought the sensation caused by this operation justified calling it "gouging the eye."

> Grover Cleveland, *Fishing and Shooting Sketches*

Protecting a Maryland Tradition

D URING the nineteenth century, the wildfowl of the Chesapeake provided more than sport for the hunters; they—particularly the canvasbacks—were a culinary delicacy for which the region became famous. The delicate flavor of the canvasbacks was attributed to the celery grass on which they fed. (This grass [*Vallisneria americana*] all but disappeared from the Susquehanna Flats as a result of severe storms in the 1950s.) Restaurants and private chefs prided themselves on their preparation of this famous dish. John Guy, who operated the famous Guy's Hotel in Baltimore, had previously operated an inn in Havre de Grace, in the 1840s; he opened his Baltimore establishment on the strength of his exceptional canvasback preparation. Indeed, the reputation of this delicacy was international, as a report in the December 3, 1875, Bel Air *Aegis and Intelligencer* evidences: "Three dozen pairs of canvass back ducks have been shipped from Baltimore to London. They are intended for Dion Boucicault, the well-known theatrical author. They were killed on the flats of Havre de Grace, on Tuesday of last week, and are said to have been choice specimens of this delicious fowl. They were packed in ice without removing the feathers, in a large market basket made expressly for the purpose." The order was received and filled by Guy's Hotel.

Cookbooks and newspapers of the day are replete with recipes for the preparation of wild duck. A very brisk fire and a very brief cooking time— twelve to twenty minutes—were universally agreed upon. The ducks were eaten rare. The *Cecil Whig* on January 17, 1863 noted, "some people are of the opinion that they should only fly through the kitchen." Once cooked, the chef removed the meat from the bird in two quick strokes and served it with the gravy that flooded from it and the traditional hominy.

This bounty was not popular with all recipients. Mid-century, when the waters of the Chesapeake swarmed with wildfowl, workers at an iron forge in Havre de Grace refused to work because they were fed on canvasback ducks instead of bacon, according to the *Aegis and Intelligencer* of March 16, 1877. A similar story was reported in the *Sun Supplement* on November 20, 1888: the contract to supply food to the workers constructing the Philadelphia, Wilmington and Baltimore Railroad bridge across the Susquehanna River contained a clause which prohibited the supplies from including wild duck more than twice a week.

Even the ducks were at times disconcerted by their own numbers as reported by the *Aegis and Intelligencer* of July 26, 1878:

A Duck Battle—We recently received from an eyewitness an account of a curious duck battle, on the Chesapeake Bay last fall. His attention was first attracted by a roaring sound, like the approach of a heavy squall, and turning his gaze upon the bay, myriads of ducks were discovered engaged in a desperate conflict. It was soon seen that they were mallards and canvasbacks, struggling for the possession of the celery fields. They finally drew off before the gentleman could decide which were the victors. The bay was strewn with quantities of duck feathers as far as the eye could reach.

The price of wild ducks in the market place reflected the supply, and, as the nineteenth century drew to a close, significantly increased prices reflected the diminished numbers of wildfowl. In the fall of 1873, ducks were more plentiful in the Upper Chesapeake than they had been in years, and at Havre de Grace blackheads sold for 25¢, redheads for 50¢, and canvasbacks for $1.25 a pair; but by the fall of 1890, canvasbacks were $4 a pair, redheads were $1.60, and blackheads were 60¢, according to newspaper reports. There was a marked decrease in the number of wildfowl by the last two decades of the century.

The decline in wildfowl was the direct result of the numbers of ducks killed by market gunners and sportsmen. An estimated 3,000 ducks were killed on the Susquehanna River on November 1, 1863, the first day of the hunting season, according to the *Sun,* despite the ongoing Civil War. Between 1870 and 1875, it was not unusual for 15,000 ducks to be killed in a single day on the Chesapeake Bay. By 1901, one-fifth of that number would have been a great score. Two famous duck hunters of Havre de Grace, William H. Dobson and John W. Leitheiser, held records, shooting 520 and 400 ducks in one day, respectively, according to the *Aegis and Intelligencer* of November 14, 1890. An old resident of Havre de Grace gave the most chilling account of the slaughter. He confessed that, in order to make his duck shooting pay when there was an overabundance of ducks, he shot canvasbacks, picked and sold their feathers, and threw the ducks to the hogs.

From the middle of the nineteenth century, the joy of the sport and the enjoyment of its delicious fruits were increasingly affected by the results of overshooting, but few understood that the excesses would ultimately lead to a severe decline in the number of wildfowl. The continuing decline in wild ducks was evidenced in newspaper reports and in ducking journal entries as the century progressed.

Many a sportsman lamented the decline in ducks over the course of his hunting career. Sportsmen blamed the market gunners, remissness in enforcement of the wildfowl laws, and practices such as night shooting with big guns while the ducks were trying to feed. In *American Duck Shooting,* George Bird Grinnell concluded that neither the market shooter nor the nonprofessional gunner had sufficient self-control to stop shooting when he had killed his fair share of birds, but instead continued to shoot as long as the fowl flew.

The scarcity of ducks was also reflected in the decline in the number of ducks a market gunner could bag in a day. In a November 1888 article entitled "Decrease In Ducks: Havoc On the Susquehanna," the *Sun* reported that a market gunner who could bag a dozen canvasbacks, after a hard day's shooting, was lucky. The newspaper attributed the decline to the work of an army of sportsmen and the deceptive devices, such as sinkboxes and bushwhack boats, which they employed. In January 1880, the *Havre de Grace Republican* suggested that those who relied on the gunning of wildfowl for a living, as did many residents of that city, should seek more reliable and profitable employment.

Some sportsmen recognized the danger which overshooting posed to this wonderful natural resource, and they championed the enforcement of wildfowl legislation. By 1874, a group of sportsmen had formed the Maryland Association for the Protection and Preservation of Game and Fish. In October of 1874, the association, of which George S. Brown, whose family owned Marshy Point, served as president, offered a reward of $50 for information leading to the conviction of any person violating legislation regarding the shooting of ducks from sneak boats. Their efforts were not always successful, as is seen from this report in the *Sun,* November 15, 1887: "Constable Grace, of Highlandtown, surprised last Sunday night at Carroll Island two night gunners from Philadelphia. One, named William Bachtel, aimed a cocked gun at the officer, who, after a struggle, took it from him. Bachtel was arrested, but his companion escaped. Officer Grace took him to Havre de Grace, where he was arraigned before Judge Charsee. Wm. M. Marine appeared for the accused, and Judge Charsee dismissed the charge. The arrest was made upon complaints from the Carroll Island Ducking Club of Baltimore."

Gunning clubs also regulated their own members. The rules of a Havre de Grace ducking club in the 1880s granted its members, who gunned from the yacht *Rough Ashlar,* the privilege of taking only four pair of ducks from the boat for a day's shooting but not more than one pair of canvasbacks or two pair of redheads.

The history of efforts to conserve our native waterfowl through legislation reflects the competing interests and various regional attitudes that affected attempts to preserve wildfowl. (See "Legislative Time Line" after this chapter.) Early on, Maryland was one of the nation's leaders in enacting conservation legislation. As early as 1832, concern about the depletion of the wildfowl population resulted in the Maryland General Assembly's enacting a law prohibiting shooting at wildfowl in the night time, except from land, in the waters of "Swann creek, Spisutie narrows, Rumney creek, Bush river and Gunpowder river, in Harford County" and banned shooting at any time in those waters from any boat with a gun that could not be conveniently fired at arm's length without a rest. Similar legislation applicable to the Potomac River was enacted that same year, regarding the killing of wildfowl that, according to the preamble to the act, were "in danger of being wholly destroyed or driven from the waters of the State." By 1837, similar protections were enacted for the waters of Cecil, Kent, and Queen Anne's Counties, including the Susquehanna and Wye rivers, and for the waters of the Patuxent and Wicomico Rivers. Penalties included the forfeiture of the offending gun or boat or both. In Cecil, Kent, and Queen Anne's Counties, if the offending party was a slave, the penalty was "any number of lashes, not exceeding thirty-nine, that may be ordered by the justice."

By 1844, two separate acts were passed to "preserve ducks," one pertaining to birds in the Sassafras, Elk, and Bohemia Rivers in Kent and Cecil Counties and the other to those in the Bush and Gunpowder Rivers in Baltimore and Harford Counties. The former prohibited shooting ducks from a boat of "less than 10 tons burthen," the latter from a boat of less than "30 tons burthen" at night, and the penalties extended to those who supplied the boat or gun or purchased the illegally procured duck.

These early legislative efforts were directed at curtailing some of the more unsavory hunting methods, such as sneaking up on the ducks in small boats as they rested in their feeding grounds at night and using large guns that killed large numbers at one firing. It was impossible to quietly approach the resting ducks in a boat of "30 tons burthen." Other provisions limited hunting to residents of Maryland; nonresidents were prohibited from shooting at wildfowl in the Sinepuxent Bay, Worcester County.

Some counties were far more progressive than others. By 1854, Baltimore, Kent, and Anne Arundel Counties had all prohibited the use of sink boats, sneak boats, or "floats" (sinkboxes), but the use of these vessels was not prohibited elsewhere in the state. In 1849, Kent County went so far as to prohibit the use of decoy ducks.

Other provisions enacted were directed more toward preferring one group of hunters over others—for example, gunning from a boat along the ducking shore of a person owning land on the Bush or Gunpowder River was also prohibited by the 1842 law, and an 1838 law prohibited boats with guns aboard from operating within fifty yards of a blind for shooting ducks in certain waters in Somerset County. The informant received one-half of the fine imposed for the latter infraction.

These early efforts at conservation were not necessarily popular. In 1845, it was "represented to the General Assembly, by the petition of a number of citizens of this State, that it is almost impossible to kill any ducks in the Elk River with ordinary ducking guns," and, in response, the legislature amended the earlier law and permitted the use of any gun or boat on the Elk River in Cecil County, provided a license was obtained.

Until 1860, the protective legislation was piecemeal; there were no provisions of statewide application. The first statewide provisions, which were enacted in that year, prohibited shooting wildfowl bedded in flocks from any vessel or from a booby blind, a floating artificial point, located over

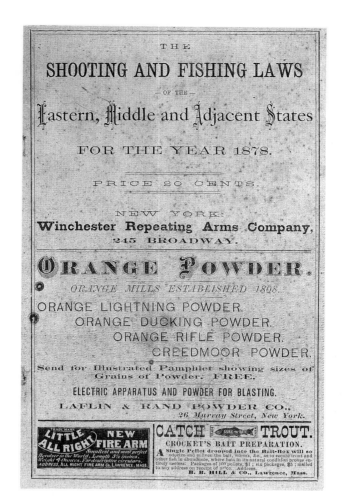

In 1878, the Winchester Repeating Company published *The Sporting and Fishing Laws of the Eastern, Middle and Adjacent States*. It included ads for not just Winchesters but cartridge companies, gun dealers, gunpowder companies, and shot manufacturers.

100 yards from the shore. Only citizens of the counties bordering on the water and those to whom they extended the privilege were permitted to shoot from a vessel at wildfowl flying about their feeding grounds, *provided* the vessel was not a sink boat or sneak boat. This severely limited the use of sink boats and sneak boats in all counties. The law provided for the seizure and forfeiture of the vessel, guns, decoy ducks, tackle, furniture, and apparel on board the vessel. At the same time, shooting with a large gun and night shooting remained banned in Anne Arundel and Kent Counties, and Kent County continued the ban on the use of duck decoys which had been enacted in 1849.

The 1860 law received strong support from some quarters. In September of 1860, John D. Smith of Spesutia Island wrote to Robert F. McGaw, father of the famous decoy maker of the same name, who then owned what was known as the Upper Farm on that island. In the letter he forwarded copies of the new ducking law and requested that McGaw collect money from their neighbors on Spesutia Island, to be used to support the strict enforcement of the law. The Smith family had once owned the entire island and still occupied portions of it.

Other hunters, discontented with the 1860 provisions against shooting ducks bedded in flocks, engaged in such practices as whipping or beating the waters or making noise on the deck of a boat with clogs or wooden shoes, all with the purpose of driving wildfowl from their feeding or roosting grounds into the sights of the hunters' guns. The General Assembly reacted in 1870 by banning these practices in Queen Anne's, Kent, Caroline, and Harford Counties.

In 1872, the General Assembly reverted to a regional approach to conservation and exempted the area in the northern reaches of Harford and Cecil Counties known as the Susquehanna Flats from the prohibitions of the 1860 act. Instead, the new provisions established for the Flats a hunting season from November 1 to March 31 and limited hunting to three days per week, but they revoked the prohibition against the use of a sinkbox or sneak boat, provided a license was obtained. They did, however, prohibit hunters gunning from a vessel from using big or swivel guns or shooting within one-half mile of the shoreline, and night gunning was prohibited.

This legislation also established the ducking police, who operated in Cecil and Harford Counties to enforce the provisions of the law. An earlier attempt at the enforcement of hunting laws by oyster police had been met with great displeasure, as this letter to the editor of the *Aegis and Intelligencer* of March 22, 1872, expresses:

Dublin, March, 1872

Mr. Editor: I am pleased to see that our Legislature has repealed the odious and oppressive law of 1870, in regard to shooting wild fowl in the head waters of the Chesapeake bay, and passed an act which will give the gunners of Havre de Grace and elsewhere the right to gun on quite a large field, by obtaining a license. The repealed act was tyrannical and oppressive, and was a great disadvantage to the citizens of Havre, without adding either to the honor, dignity or interest of the State. The citizens of Havre will be no longer annoyed with the old oystershell gun boat or the oyster police force, but they can now shoot the delicious canvasback without fear of the gallant navy. The citizens of our thriving little city deserve great credit for their forbearance in submitting to the arbitrary provisions of the late oppressive act, and have shown themselves to be a law-abiding people. MARS [the pseudonym of A. W. Scarborough].

The first ducking police were named in the 1872 statute. H. J. Poplar of Havre de Grace, kin to the famous wing shot and decoy carver Jess Poplar, and John Mahan patrolled the Harford County side of the Flats. Benjamin Dye, a famous decoy maker and one of the founders of the Cecil County style of carving, held the ducking police position on the Cecil County side of the Flats. A noteworthy later ducking policeman, from Havre de Grace, was Captain William E. Moore. Moore was the captain of the famous sloop yacht *Reckless* and the individual most responsible for the decoy painting style of R. Madison Mitchell. Madison Mitchell's father, Robert H. Mitchell, was a ducking policeman in 1888, and William Barnes, father of Samuel T. Barnes, another famous decoy maker, patrolled

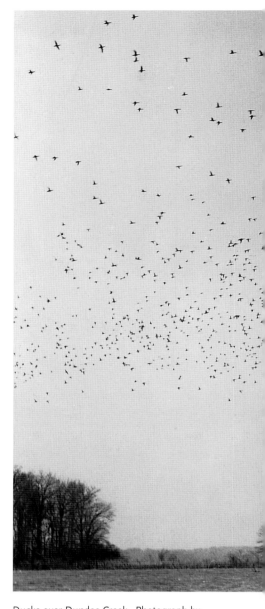

Ducks over Dundee Creek. Photograph by W. Bryant Tyrrell taken from Sandy Point looking toward Grace's Quarter, February 15, 1937.

the Flats in 1890. Sam Barnes eventually followed in his father's footsteps and in 1923 was sworn in to take his position.

Robert F. McGaw, Sr., was sworn in as a special ducking policeman in 1890. In 1920, Scott Jackson of Charlestown in Cecil County, another noteworthy carver, was also admitted to the force. And in 1929, William B. Mauldin, responsible for introducing Madison Mitchell to the use of cork for his black ducks, took the oath of office in Havre de Grace. Other familiar names among the ducking police include Ross Watson of Chesapeake City, father of Milton Watson, Elwood Heisler from Charlestown, whose relatives had been guides and professional gunners for generations, and Bennett H. Keen from Havre de Grace, whose family was long associated with the Spesutia Island Rod and Gun Club.

The legalization of the sinkbox or boat and sneak boat in the Susquehanna Flats led to the legalization of the sinkbox once again in a number of counties over the ensuing ten years. By 1882, Dorchester, Talbot, Queen Anne's, Cecil, Kent, and Anne Arundel Counties all permitted the use of the sinkbox to some extent. Shooting was limited to three or four days per week and the shooting day was shortened to comprehend the period from one hour prior to sunset to a half-hour after sunset. Some felt that this restricted only law-abiding citizens and that the best shooting was lost as a result. The writer of this entry in the journal of the gunning scow *Rough Ashlar* obviously held this view:

November 3, 1884

Beautiful morning and plenty of ducks about. Got into box at 7 o'clock. Wind light N.E. Do not think the new law a wise change as all the best shooting was lost except by those boats that broke the law and went out the day before. Think the hour of starting should be 4 o'clock.

Canvas Back	1
Red head	10
Black head	85
Bald pate	4
Marsh	8
Total	108

In an about face, and apparently at the behest of the Kent County delegation, the General Assembly in 1882 repealed the longstanding prohibition against the use of decoy ducks in that county, as well as the 1860 act's prohibition against noncitizens' shooting from a boat at wildfowl flying about their feeding grounds, as it applied to that county.

Only Baltimore and Harford Counties acted to further limit the use of the sinkbox. In 1882, any use of the sinkbox, sneak boat, or float was banned in Baltimore County and that portion of Harford County exclusive of the Susquehanna Flats. In 1888, they were joined by Cecil County in banning the trapping of wildfowl in nets in the waters of the Chesapeake in those counties.

Conservation began as a local effort. The earliest conservation provision enacted by the General Assembly applied to only a few counties. As the nineteenth century drew to a close, laws of statewide application became more restrictive and most of the local provisions enacted by the General Assembly were directed toward exempting a particular county from a state law. At the end of the century, local interests continued to control the progress of conservation efforts, but they hindered rather than promoted conservation. Addressing this situation, the preamble to an 1898 state law providing for a closed hunting season and banning the use of big guns and the practice of frightening wild ducks from their feeding or roosting grounds stated, "It is desired to secure, as far as practicable, greater uniformity in the laws of this State governing the preservation and protection of birds and game animals." Local interests apparently won the day, however, as the concluding section of the act exempted the Susquehanna Flats and nineteen counties, including all of those on the Chesapeake Bay, from the provisions of the act to the extent that the state law was inconsistent with their local laws.

The ducking police had been operating in Harford and Cecil Counties since 1872. Legislation enacted in 1896 provided for the appointment of a state game warden and deputy game wardens, to provide more vigorous enforcement of Maryland's game and fish laws. A 1914 act established a chief game warden for Harford County, to have general charge over all game wardens appointed for the county under that or any other act. One of the most respected of Harford's deputy game wardens was Frank Gowan. Gowan had, since 1892, been gamekeeper at the Cadwalader property, which comprised some 7,000 acres of the Gunpowder River game district. The Cadwalader property was the site of several gunning clubs, including the San Domingo Farm Club. Gowan served as a game warden from 1896 until the government took over the land for the creation of Edgewood Arsenal in 1917. Other wardens included: Harry Lawder, Havre de Grace, 1923; C. Maslin, Havre de Grace, 1924; decoy maker Sommerville Wilson, Havre de Grace, 1923; Walter T. Jackson, Havre de Grace, 1924; R. H. Lighthausser, Havre de Grace, 1925; and decoy maker Jesse Berkentein, Aberdeen, 1928.

The Boyer family of Harford County relate an account of their efforts to enforce waterfowl legislation. In the late 1880s, Henry H. Boyer moved his family from Baltimore to Perryman, on the Bush River. At that time, the Bush River area would most certainly have been a waterfowler's dream. Large flocks of many species of waterfowl rafted within view of the Boyer home, near the Harford County seat. The family was in the business of canning and packing oysters, fruits, and vegetables at their Baltimore office and factory, located at West Falls Avenue and Boston Street.

The Boyers' account begins with the concerns of their grandfather, Henry H. Boyer, over a big gun that echoed periodically off the shores near the Boyers' riverfront home. The game wardens were called repeatedly, but no evidence of the gun was ever found. As the tale unfolds, a Mr. Payhill (or "Pay-Hell" as the respectable residents of the Bush River Neck were fond of calling him) had made an arrangement with the bridge tender on the Pennsylvania Railroad to signal the nefarious night hunter with his signal light if the game wardens were in his area. Payhill, who used his large gun to fire into resting flocks, would immediately lower the gun into the river if the game wardens drew near. A line with a large cork float attached was tied to the gun. The line and cork, anchored by a large block of rock salt, would sink to the bottom of the river. When the game wardens inspected the area after Mr. Boyer's report, nothing would be found; but shortly after the game wardens had left the scene, the rock salt would dissolve and the cork float would rise to the surface and signal the gun's location. Mr. Payhill would then retrieve his gun and ready himself for the next evening's shoot.

With Boyer's persistence and the help of Lady Luck and the game wardens, the big gun was finally located and confiscated. Payhill warned all involved that the train which transported the captured gun to Baltimore would be stopped en route, and he declared that Boyer's life was in danger. When the train with the confiscated gun on board stopped at the Edgewood Station, Payhill and companion did climb aboard, but much to their dismay, they found the gun protected by armed guards in the baggage car. His attempt to reclaim his prized possession was foiled on the spot. Shortly thereafter, a mysterious fire did destroy a major barn on the Boyer farm; Payhill was suspected, but no charges were ever brought against him. The big gun was displayed in the Federal Building in Baltimore as a warning to other illegal hunters, and Boyer was protected by federal agents on his daily train trips to his packing business.

The gun survived only a short time, being lost in the Great Fire of Baltimore in 1904. Payhill lived only a few years beyond its demise. The Boyer family spent many happy and peaceful years enjoying the magnificent flocks of migrating waterfowl from the shores of their Bush River home.

The struggle between local interests and the state's interest in preserving the once plentiful wildfowl continued through the first quarter of the next century. In 1910, the legislature enacted a comprehensive statute, the most stringent law to date, which prohibited killing or shooting at wildfowl from any boat of any description within the state. Dead or wounded wildfowl could be pursued, shot over or gathered from boats propelled by oars only. The boats, guns, and other paraphernalia of violators were confiscated. The law also prohibited the disturbance of wildfowl in their feeding or roosting grounds, shooting wildfowl on Sundays or at night, shooting wildfowl with a rifle, a big gun, or a swivel gun, and the use of dynamite to capture or kill wildfowl. Properly licensed sneak boats used for shooting wildfowl on the flats of the Susquehanna were excepted from this law.

Still struggling to achieve uniformity in wildfowl laws, the legislature included in the 1910 act a provision that all state and local laws and parts of laws inconsistent with the provisions of the 1910 law were repealed. But the struggle continued. In 1914, the waters of the Chesapeake north of a line drawn from Howells Point in Kent County to Stony Point in Harford County and north of a line drawn from Spesutia Island in Harford County to Turkey Point in Cecil County were excepted from the prohibition against gathering wounded or dead ducks in a boat equipped with sail or engine. Hunting from duly licensed sneak and push boats was once again permitted south of the Susquehanna Flats. On the Flats, motor boats running with the wind while shooting over decoys or retrieving wildfowl were also permitted.

Other efforts at uniformity were more successful. In 1916, the legislature enacted statewide bag limits—not more than twenty-five wild waterfowl per day per person. This was a radical change from the practices of many sportsmen, as the *Eildon Ducking Club Journal* for April 6, 1892, testifies: "Mundy and J. C. Day shot in Johnson Cove and killed 112 ducks before

A group of bluebills hanging on the side of the Smith house on Spesutia Island in 1900. There are 160 ducks in this picture.

10 a.m. . . . Wind southwest overcast. This makes a total of 279 ducks for two morning shoots. Both great days and breaks the record." The 1916 law also shortened the ducking season to the period from November 1 to March 15 throughout the state.

At the end of 1916, the Migratory Bird Treaty between the United States and Great Britain was signed; migratory waterfowl, including brant, wild ducks, geese, and swans, came under its protection. In 1918, the Congress ratified the treaty and passed the Migratory Bird Treaty Act, effectively removing some aspects of the struggle between competing interests from the hands of Maryland's legislature. That act stringently limited the hunting or killing of migratory birds. Regulations eliminated the spring season and limited the open season in Maryland to the period from November 1 to January 31. The birds could be taken only by gun, of not larger than 10-gauge, from the land or water, with the aid of dogs and decoys; blinds or floating devices were permitted, other than airplanes, powerboats, or any boat under sail. The purchase or sale of wildfowl, except under permits for strictly scientific or propagating purposes, was absolutely prohibited. This ended the careers of the market gunners.

Maryland retained the right to enact legislation to give further protection to wildfowl and continued to legislate for their protection. The state's efforts were in part funded by the creation of the state hunting license in 1918. In 1927, the General Assembly enacted "The Game Law," comprehensive legislation that paralleled the requirements of federal regulations and incorporated earlier provisions of the general and local game laws into one law. The Susquehanna Flats continued to receive different treatment and were separately addressed by the new law.

The sinkbox and sneak boat once again survived, but to a limited extent. The sneak boat was banned except on the Susquehanna Flats and in certain waters of Cecil County. Sinkboxes or boats were permitted on the Susquehanna Flats, in certain waters of Cecil County, in certain waters of Kent County, and in Anne Arundel and Talbot Counties, and in the waters of the Isle of Wight and Chincoteague Bays in Worcester County.

Not until 1930 did the federal regulations become more stringent, decreasing the bag limit to fifteen ducks. The next year the season for shooting ducks was shortened to thirty days, November 16 to December 15. By 1935, the bag limit was reduced to ten ducks. However, it was the banning of the sinkbox in 1935 and the requirement that bushwhack rigs not be set more than 100 feet from the natural shore nor more than 100 feet from natural vegetation that changed the nature of ducking in Maryland forever. The final blow came in 1936 when canvasback shooting was banned on the Susquehanna Flats. No more did wealthy sports have a "ducker's paradise" on the Susquehanna Flats.

Legislative Time Line

References by chapter are to the dated volumes of the *Laws of Maryland*.

1832   Chap. 134   Prohibited night shooting on the water and shooting with a large gun from any boat on the Potomac River and its tributary streams.

1832   Chap. 161   Prohibited night shooting and shooting with a large gun in the waters of Swann Creek, Spisutie Narrows, Rumney Creek, Bush River, and Gunpowder River in Harford County.

1837   Chap. 10   Prohibited night shooting on the waters of Cecil, Kent, and Queen Anne's Counties, including the Susquehanna and Wye Rivers, and shooting with a large gun from a boat at any time.

1837   Chap. 100   Prohibited the navigating of any open boat with a fowling piece on board in the waters of Smith's Island and its vicinity in Somerset County within fifty yards of any blind for shooting fowl.

1837   Chap. 291   Prohibited night shooting except from land or a blind fixed on some bar, and shooting with a large gun on the waters of the Patuxent and Wicomico Rivers and their tributaries.

1841   Chap. 260   Prohibited gunning in the Bush and Gunpowder Rivers from a vessel of less than 30 tons burthen, except with a small gun in the daytime not immediately along the ducking shores of any person.

1842   Chap. 30   Prohibited nonresidents of the state from shooting at wildfowl or taking oysters or terrapins in the waters of Sinepuxent Bay in Worcester County.

1842   Chap. 61   Prohibited persons not citizens of the state or the owner of property on the Potomac River from shooting ducks from a vessel within the waters of the Potomac or any creeks or branches connected with it.

1843 Chap. 302 Prohibited shooting ducks from any vessel of less than 10 tons burthen in the waters of the Sassafras, Elk, and Bohemia Rivers or any connected creeks or branches.

1845 Chap. 266 Permitted citizens of Cecil County, after obtaining a license, to gun for and kill ducks in the Elk River with any gun or boat, due to the impossibility of killing any ducks in the Elk River with ordinary ducking guns.

1849 Chap. 305 Prohibited the use of decoy ducks, sink boats, sneak boats, craft, or floats in the waters of Chester and Sassafras Rivers and the Chesapeake Bay, and their tributary streams, bordering on Kent County, while engaged in shooting wild ducks; provided for the forfeiture of the decoys, boats, and guns.

1853 Chap. 190 Prohibited the use of sink boats, sneak boats or floats in the waters of Back and Middle Rivers, Dundee, Salt Petre, and Seneca Creeks and their tributary streams in Baltimore County while engaged in shooting wild ducks.

1854 Chap. 3 Prohibited the use of sink boats, sneak boats, or floats in any of the rivers, creeks, and waters of Anne Arundel County while engaged in shooting wildfowl.

1859 Maryland Code, Article 97, "Wild Fowl," contained no statewide provisions but rather only the provisions of public local laws prohibiting gunning from any vessel on the Potomac; gunning in Cecil, Kent, Queen Anne's, Harford, and Baltimore Counties from a vessel at night or from a vessel at any time with a large gun, and gunning from a vessel immediately along a ducking shore of a person owning land on the Bush and Gunpowder Rivers.

1860 Chap. 109 Enacted provisions with statewide application prohibiting shooting waterfowl bedded in flocks, either on their feeding or roosting grounds or elsewhere from any vessel, shooting from any booby blind or artificial point over 100 yards from shore, and shooting waterfowl flying about their feeding grounds or elsewhere from a vessel, except by citizens of bordering counties from other than sink or sneak boats. Also provided for the forfeiture to the arresting officer of the vessel together with the tackle, furniture, and apparel on board.

1860 Public local laws in Baltimore, Anne Arundel, Kent, and Talbot Counties continued to prohibit the use of sink boats, sneak boats, and floats; Anne Arundel and Kent continued to ban night gunning on the water and the use of a large gun on a vessel; Kent banned the use of decoy ducks; and Somerset banned boats with guns within 100 yards of a blind for shooting fowl in certain areas. There were no other public local laws in effect.

1867   Chap. 41   Prohibited whipping or beating the waters of Romney Creek in Harford County to the effect of driving or frightening wild ducks or waterfowl from their feeding or roosting grounds.

1870   Chap. 231   Prohibited lashing or beating the waters or making noise on the deck of a boat with clogs or wooden shoes within the limits of Queen Anne's, Kent, Caroline, and Harford Counties for the purpose of driving or frightening waterfowl from their feeding or roosting grounds.

1870   Chap. 296   Authorized head of the oyster police force to detail a portion of his force to visit and cruise about the Susquehanna and other rivers of the state to enforce the provisions of law relating to wildfowl.

1872   Chap. 54   Enacted a separate wildfowl law for that portion of the waters of the Chesapeake Bay lying north of a line beginning at Turkey Point, Cecil County, westward to one-half mile north of Spesutia Island, westward to the shores of Harford County near Oakington. Established a season from November 1 to March 31; banned night gunning; banned shooting from a vessel within one-half mile of any shore in Cecil and Harford Counties; banned gunning from a vessel with a big or swivel gun; limited gunning to three days per week during the season; required a license to operate a sinkbox or sneak boat; established ducking police in Cecil and Harford Counties, and appointed John Mahan and Henry J. Poplar of Harford County and Benjamin Die [Dye] of Cecil County as the first ducking police.

1872   Chap. 442   Permitted the shooting of waterfowl from sink boats in or over the waters of the Choptank River within the limits of Dorchester County on Tuesdays, Thursdays, and Saturdays by citizens or any person to whom a citizen may extend the privilege.

1876   Chap. 45   Permitted the shooting of wildfowl from sinkboxes in Talbot County by bona fide citizens of the county three days per week.

1878   Chap. 292   Permitted the shooting of wildfowl from sinkboxes in the waters of the Elk and Bohemia Rivers and their tributaries in Cecil County by bona fide citizens on four days a week from November 1 to March 31 with a license.

1880   Chap. 27   Prohibited lashing or beating the waters at certain points on the Elk and Bohemia Rivers to drive fish into a net when persons were engaged in gunning with decoys or gunning from the bridge over the Bohemia.

1880   Chap. 42   Permitted the shooting of wildfowl from sinkboxes in certain parts of the Sassafras River in Cecil and Kent Counties by bona fide citizens of the county from November 1 to March 31, three days per week.

1880   Chap. 160   Prohibited shooting wildfowl between April 10 and November, use of nets to capture wild waterfowl, and night shooting by firelight in Worcester County.

1880   Chap. 194   Prohibited beating the waters in Romney Creek in Harford County to frighten or drive wild ducks from their feeding or roosting grounds.

1880   Chap. 370   Permitted the citizens of Queen Anne's County to shoot wildfowl from sinkboxes in the waters of Queen Anne's County with a license.

1882   Chap. 96   Permitted the shooting of ducks or other wildfowl from the shore over decoys in Kent County.

1882   Chap. 169   Repealed the prohibition against the shooting of wildfowl flying about their feeding grounds from a vessel in Kent County.

1882   Chap. 204   Permitted the shooting of wildfowl from sinkboxes in certain parts of the Sassafras River in Cecil and Kent Counties by bona fide citizens of those counties from November 1 to March 31 four days per week with a license.

1882   Chap. 278   Prohibited the use of sink boats, sneak boats, floats, and big or swivel guns for the purpose of shooting at wild ducks in the waters of Harford and Baltimore Counties or of the Chesapeake Bay adjacent to them, up to the middle of the Bay, and prohibited any act intended to frighten wild ducks from their feeding or roosting grounds, the location of a booby blind greater than 100 yards from the shore in those waters, and night shooting, excepting the Susquehanna Flats.

1884   Chap. 506   Prohibited the shooting of wildfowl from any craft in or over the waters within one-quarter mile of any shore on the Susquehanna Flats in Harford County or Cecil County.

1886   Chap. 215   Authorized the shooting of teal ducks, mallards, black ducks, baldpates, and all other ducks known as marsh ducks other than by swivel or big gun from August 15 to October 1 on those waters of the Chesapeake Bay known as the Susquehanna Flats.

1886   Chap. 437   Extended to land owners whose land bordered on the Chesapeake Bay in the Susquehanna Flats the right to select a gunning point on that shore each year and have exclusive right to station crafts, to gun, and to set decoys within a fixed distance from shore.

1888   Chap. 390   Prohibited any attempt to take, trap, or catch wild-fowl in nets of any kind in the waters of the Chesapeake or its tributaries within Cecil, Harford, and Baltimore Counties north of a line drawn from the most southerly point of Cecil County to the most southerly point of Baltimore County.

1888   Chap. 466   Permitted the citizens of Charles County to shoot wild waterfowl from sinkboxes in the waters of Charles County.

1892   Chap. 582   Restricted the use of a booby or bush blind in Anne Arundel County on the Severn and Magothy Rivers to certain days and required a license for a booby blind on the South River.

1896   Chap. 293   Provided for the appointment of a state game warden and deputy game wardens to provide more vigorous enforcement of Maryland's game and fish laws.

1898   Chap. 206   The preamble to this act stated that it was based on the desire to secure greater uniformity in the laws governing the protection of bird and game animals. The act established a November 1 through April 10 hunting season, prohibited the use of big or swivel guns and frightening ducks from their feeding or roosting grounds, but exempted the Susquehanna Flats and nineteen counties, including those on the Chesapeake Bay to the extent their local laws were inconsistent. The act also prohibited the buying or selling of wild ducks, geese, or swan in Baltimore outside of the hunting season.

1904   Chap. 498   Authorized the Hooper's Island Gunning Club in Dorchester County to shoot every day but Sunday and prohibited the placement of booby blinds within 300 yards of their property.

1908   Chap. 592   Permitted residents or persons duly licensed to shoot wildfowl within Worcester County to use and shoot from bush blinds, batteries, or sinkboxes in the waters of the Isle of Wight and Chincoteague Bays.

1910   Chap. 251   Prohibited shooting at or killing any wildfowl from any boat of any description within Maryland and pursuing or gathering wounded or dead ducks in any boat propelled by or equipped with sail or engines; duly licensed sneak boats for shooting wildfowl on the Susquehanna Flats were excluded, as was shooting over or gathering wounded or dead ducks from boats propelled only by oars.

1912 Chap. 611 Extended the time for shooting wildfowl over the waters of the Chester River in Kent County to the 25th day of April.

1914 Chap. 365 Established the office of chief game warden for Harford County, to have general charge over all game wardens appointed for Harford County under this or any other act.

1914 Chap. 579 Excepted the Chesapeake north of a line drawn from Howells Point in Kent County to Stony Point in Harford County and north of a line from Spesutia in Harford County to Turkey Point in Cecil County from the prohibition against gathering wounded or dead ducks in a boat equipped with a sail or engine. Also exempted the proper use of all duly licensed sneak or push boats (flat-bottomed skiffs propelled by a push pole).

1916 Chap. 542 Prohibited shooting at or killing wildfowl in or from any boat of any description in Maryland or gathering wounded or dead ducks from any boat propelled by or equipped with sail or engines of any kind; provided that duly licensed sneak boats or push boats were permitted as was shooting over or gathering wounded or dead wildfowl from boats propelled only by oars; provided that north of a line from Turkey Point in Cecil County to Locust Point in Harford County, motor boats running with the wind while shooting over decoys or retrieving waterfowl wounded over decoys were permitted.

1916 Chap. 545 Established a bag limit for game birds—not more than twenty-five wild waterfowl in one day per person—and provided for the repeal of all laws or parts thereof inconsistent with that limit.

1916 Chap. 568 Prohibited shooting any duck, goose, swan, or brant in Maryland between March 15 and November 1.

1916 The Migratory Bird Treaty between Great Britain and the United States was signed, and migratory waterfowl, including wild ducks, brant, wild geese, and swan, came under its protection.

1918 Congress passed the Migratory Bird Treaty Act, which banned the hunting or killing of any migratory bird except as provided by regulations. Regulations eliminated the spring season and established a November 1 to January 31 hunting season. Birds could be taken only by gun, not larger than 10-gauge, from the land and water, with the aid of a dog and decoys, and from a blind or floating device other than an airplane, powerboat, or boat under sail.

1918   Chap. 468   Established an annual state hunting license, to provide funds to pay the expense of the protection of game.

1920   Chap. 510   Permitted sinkboxes for the hunting and shooting of wildfowl on the Potomac River in Charles and Prince George's Counties.

1922   Chap. 458   Authorized bona fide residents and owners of real estate of the value of $500 or more to shoot wildfowl from sinkboxes and from floating or booby blinds in the waters of the Sassafras River in Kent and Cecil from November 1 to January 31 with a license.

1924   Chap. 13   Prohibited shooting or killing wildfowl in Maryland between February 1 and October 31, restricted the size of boats used in conjunction with hunting rigs on the Susquehanna Flats to those at least 16 feet in length and 20 inches at the lowest point in height and repealed all inconsistent local and general laws.

1927   Chap. 340   Enacted as part of "The Game Law" separate provisions relating to the Susquehanna Flats.

1927   Chap. 568   Enacted "The Game Law" which repealed all general and local game laws and reenacted existing provisions with regard to pursuit of wildfowl, game wardens, bag limits, hunting season, state game license and prohibited the shipping of game out of state. The new law separately addressed the Susquehanna Flats.

1935   Federal regulations prohibited the use of the sinkbox and severely limited the use of the bushwhack boat, limiting it to use within 100 feet of shoreline at high water or within 100 feet of protruding natural growth or vegetation.

1936   Federal regulations included the canvasback and redhead ducks in the fully protected species and prohibited shooting them.

Folk Art

Duck Decoys

WHO MADE the first decoy?" Joel Barber asked this question in *Wild Fowl Decoys.* He related a tale that attributed the first "wooden stool," as the colonists called wildfowl decoys, in New York to an old man who came down from Massachusetts before the Revolutionary War. Barber concluded that, at least according to legend, the first decoy of American duck shooting came into existence before the Revolution. Certainly duck decoys were known in Massachusetts before 1776. David McCullough relates, in his wonderful biography, *John Adams,* that on September 3, 1776, when General John Sullivan of the Continental Army appeared before the Continental Congress to deliver the British request for an accommodation—clearly something less than independence—John Adams was so incensed that he took the floor and called Sullivan "a decoy duck sent to seduce Congress into renunciation of independence." Adams was a native of coastal Massachusetts and an avid hunter of waterfowl as a youth. This is certainly consistent with Barber's legend.

The use of wooden or stool ducks in the Chesapeake region did not begin until later. *The Cabinet of Natural History* published in 1830 noted that stool ducks were little used in the Chesapeake region. They were known enough by 1849, however, for the Maryland legislature to pass a law prohibiting the use of decoy ducks in the waters of the Chester and Sassafras Rivers and Chesapeake Bay bordering on Kent County.

If decoys are now considered art, they are one of America's unique contributions to that world. In *Sporting Scenes and Sundry Sketches* of J. Cypress, Jr., edited by Frank Forester and published in 1842, decoys are referred to as "stools" and described as "wooden devices of the shape, size, and complexion of the fowl you wish to subduce from the upper air. Sculptor and painter are employed in their manufacture. . . . They are miserable wooden pictures of bay birds, whose distant view brings enchantment to the living jaunters." The gunner set out decoys some 20 or 30 yards from blinds or shooting points and used them in the greatest quantity around the sinkbox. Elisha Lewis, the author of *The American Sportsman,* recommended numbers of not less than 200 and most generally 250 or more for sinkbox use. Lewis also noted that decoys made of solid blocks, if ordered during the idle season, could be had at a moderate price, ranging from $20 to $30 per hundred. A club or individual gunner would purchase an entire rig at one time; canvasbacks were always included.

WANTED TO BUY—
TWO HUNDRED AND FIFTY DECOYS,
Canvas Back and Red Heads. Address
DECOY, Sun office for three days.
The Sun, September 22, 1879.

Fortunately for those who carved these wooden fowl, decoys were often lost to the elements and required replacement and rigs were expanded. In 1868, the Seneca River Ducking Club of Baltimore County extended its shooting bar 60 yards and purchased 500 additional decoys. On March 11, 1887, the entry in the gunning log of the scow *Rough Ashlar* out of Havre de Grace recorded the results of an encounter with a "gale of wind": "we were fortunate in saving everything. *Reckless* lost half her decoys." *Reckless* and *Rough Ashlar* were both well-known gunning scows.

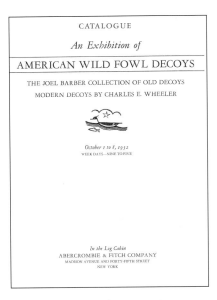

Decoy exhibition catalogue, October 1932

Pintail drake by R. Madison Mitchell, 1938

Decoys have seen decorative uses for more than eighty-five years. These cast-iron goose andirons were fashioned from the pattern of James T. Holly, Havre de Grace, Maryland, circa 1915.

Canvasback drake by George Washington Barnes, circa 1910. The account book of C. C. Pusey's store in Havre de Grace records the purchase of a group of George Washington Barnes's decoys for $9 on September 25, 1880.

A circa 1880 picture of two Havre de Grace gunners inscribed "Jack and I." They sit behind their new rig.

Canvasback drake by R. Madison Mitchell, circa 1938, an early decorative decoy

Ruddy drake pair by Benjamin Dye, circa 1880

Each decoy would have a string several feet in length attached to the breast by means of a leather thong, loop, or metal ring and staple. Attached to the other end of the string would be the anchor, a small piece of leaden pipe or a fragment of an angular stone. Eventually, these anchors were mass-produced and cast in foundries close to the hunting grounds. The arriving migrants, not knowing where to go or where to feed, would follow the example set by their wooden kinfolk, and be "apt to look at the arrival-book of the public places of 'entertainment for ducks,'" and stop where their friends were, only to be greeted by the harsh Bang! Bang! of the "obtainer of ducks under false pretences" (F. Forester, ed., *Sporting Scenes and Sundry Sketches*).

In addition to the wooden blocks or stools, the hunter's ingenuity resulted in decoys of varied form. When shooting teal, black ducks, or mallards in shallow waters and with few decoys available, a hunter might employ bunches of brush, pieces of bark, and lumps of mud to deceive the wild ducks. For swan shooting, white shirts or sheets were used with branches or sticks formed in proper positions to mimic the giant white birds. The form of decoy that seems the cruelest but the most realistic was a shot fowl positioned as naturally as possible along the shoreline or on the ice. Many times their heads were tucked under their wings to simulate a resting or sleeping fowl. But it is the wooden decoy that epitomizes American duck shooting and has now become the symbol of that sport.

Collection of decoy heads made between 1900 and 1930

My Newfoundland dog "Good Girl"

CANVASBACK DRAKE
James A. Currier, Havre de Grace, circa 1920

BLUEBILL DRAKE
William Y. Heverin, Charlestown, circa 1930

REDHEAD DRAKE
Benjamin Dye, Perryville, circa 1870, branded
E.L.B. (Edward L. Bartlett)

GOLDENEYE PAIR (male and female)
R. Madison Mitchell, Havre de Grace, circa
1948

CANVASBACK HEN
R. Madison Mitchell, Havre de Grace, circa
1938

PINTAIL DRAKE
Robert F. McGaw, Havre de Grace, circa 1940

CANVASBACK PAIR
Robert F. McGaw, Havre de Grace, circa 1925

GREEN-WING TEAL PAIR
R. Madison Mitchell, Havre de Grace, circa
1944

CANADA GOOSE
James T. Holly, Havre de Grace, circa 1915

GOOSE
maker unknown, Havre de Grace, circa 1900

BLUEBILL DRAKE
Joseph E. Dye, Havre de Grace, circa 1920

GREEN-WING TEAL DRAKE
W. Scott Jackson, Charlestown, circa 1920

SWAN DIVING DEVICE
R. Madison Mitchell, Havre de Grace, circa
1934

CANVASBACK DRAKES (high-head models)
James T. Holly, Havre de Grace, circa 1915

RUDDY DUCK DRAKE
S.D.F.C. (San Domingo Farm Club's brand),
maker unknown, Gunpowder River, circa 1880

CANVASBACK PAIR (high-neck models)
Charles Nelson Barnard, Havre de Grace,
circa 1918

BLUEBILL PAIR
Charles Nelson Barnard, Havre de Grace,
circa 1935

MALLARD DRAKE
John B. Graham, Charlestown, circa 1900

MALLARD PAIR
Robert F. McGaw, Havre de Grace, circa 1930

BLUE-WING TEAL PAIR
Robert F. McGaw, Havre de Grace, circa 1940

SWAN
R. Madison Mitchell, Havre de Grace,
circa 1938

CANVASBACK HEN (preening model)
John B. Graham, Charlestown, circa 1900

BLUEBILL DRAKES (wing ducks)
(*top*) maker unknown, Havre de Grace, circa 1900; (*bottom*) James T. Holly, Havre de Grace, circa 1900

BLACK DUCK
William Y. Heverin, Charlestown, circa 1930

CANVASBACK DRAKE
Leonard Pryor, Chesapeake City, circa 1930

SWAN
James Cockey, Stevensville, circa 1920

CANVASBACK DRAKE
John B. Graham, Charlestown, circa 1900

PINTAIL DRAKE (high-head model)
R. Madison Mitchell, Havre de Grace, 1938

BLUEBILL DRAKE
Grace's Quarter Gunning Club's brand,
James T. Holly, Havre de Grace, circa 1900

BUFFLEHEAD PAIR
maker unknown, Susquehanna Flats, circa 1905

PINTAIL PAIR
John Glen, Rock Hall, circa 1930

WIDGEON DRAKE
John Glen, Rock Hall, circa 1930

CANVASBACK DRAKE
August Heinefield, Rock Hall, circa 1920

MERGANSER PAIR
John Baker, Hooper's Island, circa 1935

CANADA GOOSE
(high-head watch goose model)
Edward Phillips, Cambridge, circa 1930

CANVASBACK DRAKE
Pied Jones, Crisfield, circa 1929

CANVASBACK DRAKE
L. Travis Ward, Crisfield, circa 1910

REDHEAD DRAKE (hollow "fat jaw" model)
Lem and Steve Ward, Crisfield, circa 1918

PINTAIL DRAKE
Lloyd J. Tyler, Crisfield, circa 1930

BLUEBILL DRAKE
Lem and Steve Ward, Crisfield, circa 1932

CANADA GOOSE
Lloyd J. Tyler, Crisfield, circa 1925

CANADA GOOSE
L. Travis Ward, Crisfield, circa 1910

CANVASBACK DRAKE (knothead model)
Lem and Steve Ward, Crisfield, circa 1929

SWAN PAIR attributed to Harry Emmords, used by the Taylor's Island Ducking and Fishing Club on the Bush River Neck in Harford County. In 1902 the club owned 20 swan decoys valued at 60 cents each.

GUNNING BOX for muzzle-loading shotgun, circa 1840, with shot bags from Merchants Shot Works and James Robertson's Lead Works of Baltimore, and a Hazard Powder Company can

SHOTGUN POWDER CANS for muzzle-loading guns, 1860 to 1920. Alexander McComas's private label appears on the bottom center can.

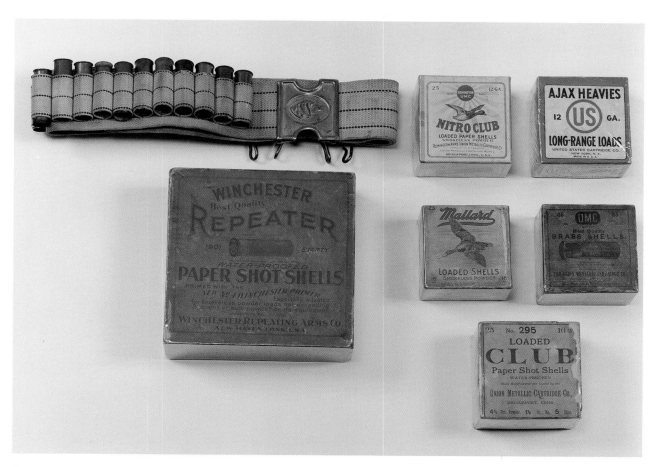

Shotgun shell boxes, circa 1901 to 1920,
for breech-loading guns

DUCK SHOOTING from a sinkbox, painted by James T. Holly, circa 1890

A BATTERY ON THE POTOMAC

SHOTGUN POWDER CANS used for large bore muzzle-loading punt guns. These English and American cans date from 1880 to 1920

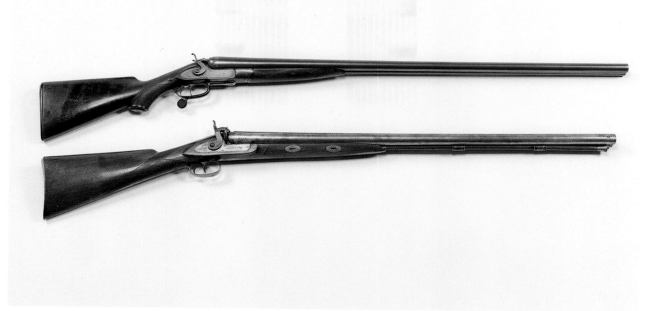

(*Top*) BREECH-LOADING 8-gauge under-lever double-barreled shotgun made by Alexander McComas, 51 South Calvert Street, Baltimore, circa 1890; and (*bottom*) an English-made 8-gauge muzzle-loading double barrel, made circa 1805

COLT 10-gauge breech-loading shotgun used on the Susquehanna Flats by decoy makers Charles Nelson Barnard and Thomas P. Barnard, circa 1890.

THE DUCK HUNTER'S ACCESSORIES: leather leg-o-mutton shotgun carrying case made in Baltimore, circa 1890, and wooden shotgun shell carrying case for sixty-six 10-gauge shells, circa 1890

CHARLES NELSON BARNARD'S TOOLBOX, miniatures, head patterns, and the last of the high-heads owned by his son

In the Shop of Paul Gibson

N THE MID-1960s I began to acquire decoys with the unrelenting enthusiasm that is shared by so many new collectors. In those days I, like hundreds of unguided souls, headed out to accumulate rather than collect. The concept was to acquire as many decoys as possible—anything that vaguely resembled a duck was fair game.

It was at about this time that I was to meet and become lasting friends with some individuals who would change my direction in decoy collecting, and ultimately, my life. In 1968, R. Madison Mitchell, Jr., came to work for the county government where I too was employed. When Mitch was assigned an office, one of the first decorative items he placed in it was a photograph of his father holding one of his decoys. The photograph, of course, caught my attention and, based on my keen interest, Mitch arranged to take me to Havre de Grace to meet his father and purchase my first new Mitchell decoys.

I will always recall those first Mitchell decoys: I paid $6 each for ducks and $8 each for geese. Home from that visit, I quickly gathered from my earlier accumulation the decoys that most closely resembled my new decoys and traveled back to Havre de Grace. Mr. Mitchell carefully examined those decoys, looking at each one, identifying his and setting aside those made by others. The decoys seemed so very similar to me that I couldn't distinguish them. He then proceeded to give me my first lesson in decoy identification, pointing out subtle differences between decoys by the various Havre de Grace carvers.

Many of the examples that he set aside he identified as being made by Paul Gibson. I loaded up my decoys and headed across town to Ontario Street, to the shop of Mr. Gibson. As I opened the side yard gate and started toward the shop, a big, burly man opened the kitchen door and asked if he could help me. I identified myself and found that I was in the presence of none other than Paul Gibson. This congenial gentleman invited me into the kitchen to meet his wife, Mae, where I joined them for coffee and Mrs. Gibson's homemade cookies. That first visit was to be one of many over the years to come. Paul and Mae would go out of their way as hosts to me and my wife, and especially my young son, John. Saturday morning was always a good time to visit, and many hours were spent sitting on a stool in front of Paul's carving bench or in a chair facing him as he painted decoys.

During these visits, he shared pleasant recollections of his life in and around Havre de Grace. Paul was born in 1902, one of five children in his family. His father, Hugh, a waterman, market gunner, and woodworker, died in 1904. Paul left school at an early age to help support the family. His association with old-time hunters, watermen, and decoy makers influenced him, and under Samuel T. Barnes's tutelage, Paul carved his very first decoy, a miniature canvasback, at age thirteen. Paul's stories, told as he worked about the shop, related his experiences duck shooting on his beloved Susquehanna Flats and gunning for rabbits in the River Hills. Paul much preferred bushwhacking for canvasbacks than gunning from his sinkbox.

Over the years I watched Paul sign his decoys; he always signed each one the same way, "Paul Gibson, Maker and Painter, Havre de Grace, Md." This signature, I was to learn, indicated that no one else had worked on the decoy—it was marked as Paul's work alone. Paul sawed the block, turned the body, carved the head, spoke shaved the body, sanded it, attached the head, and then primed it, painted it, and floated and weighted it.

From the moment visitors entered on the Gibson property, they would be struck by the fastidiousness of the lawn, the house, and the garden. The same attention to order was evident throughout the shop. Paul prided himself on making as good a product as he could possibly make. His workmanship was evident in his decoys, the furniture he made, the boats he built and repaired, and the novel items he turned out. I have a bird feeder that Paul made in approximately 1940. It is designed to last at least 100 years, with the proper care.

Paul, in his one-man operation, set aside specific areas in his rambling two-story shop for each step in his decoy making process. His attention to order immediately caught the eye of a visitor to his workshop. The long workbench (where the famous Maryland photographer Aubrey Bodine captured Paul in 1940) was arranged in such a fashion that everything was placed for easy access: spoke shaves, draw knives, and carving knives each had their own reserved space. Two large windows above the workbench flooded the room with natural light. Placed in the windows were head patterns for the various species that Paul carved. Attached to the bench were wooden vices to hold decoy bodies.

One of my favorite spots was to the left of the workbench. There hung a series of five drawers from a by-gone Havre de Grace apothecary shop. The porcelain labels on the drawers were marked in Latin: Thymus, Prunivirg, Nux Vomic, etc. Then, next to their former names, Paul had attached sample nails indicating what had now replaced the drawers' original contents. As if that was not enough to identify the new use for those drawers, Paul had attached to the drawers' exposed sides small decoy body sections decorated with his very best paint. These sections were slender slabs left over from decoy bodies that had been made into ornamental wall plaques in the 1940s.

Paul Gibson at his workbench in Havre de Grace

Black duck exhibiting Gibson's finest scratch-painting technique

In that same bright room with the long workbench were Paul's lathe, band saws, table saws, and sanders. Wood dust rested on the window mullions and the floor below like a soft dry snow. Out the door to the left was his sawmill, while a small door to the right led to his lead melting and iron working shop. Out of the main door and into the garage, a visitor would head up the stairs to the paint loft. Paul would warn each guest to watch his or her head on the low beam, but somehow I managed to get a minor concussion about every other visit to the shop. Paul's paint loft was heated

Canada goose, circa 1940

by a large wood stove, which warmed the occupant thoroughly on a cold winter day. There is no heat more pleasant than that from a wood stove, and when the fuel is white pine spiced with cedar from decoy scraps, it seemed even more so.

The paint loft held not only the painting necessities—paints, brushes, a painting table, and drying racks—but also other bits of nostalgia from a waterman's life. Here rested Paul's skulling oars, two sets of loom oars, boat lights, anchors, and rope. From the paint loft, one step led up to a large bright room with a long row of windows and an additional drying rack. This room was usually reserved for the larger ducks, and geese. This drying room was where Paul had placed his weighting table. Paul floated every decoy in a tub, then moved the bird onto a padded table where the ballast weight would be attached. A formal air was given to this room, not just by the order maintained on the drying rack, but also by the presence of Paul's fire chief's uniform from the Edgewood Arsenal Fire Department hanging to the right of the rack.

Paul's production of decoys over the years was not enormous. He made a high-quality product, and that took time. A decoy buyer who was willing to wait would ultimately receive a decoy that would last. Paul made Canada geese, canvasbacks, redheads, bluebills, baldpates, mallards, black ducks, blue-wing teal, green-wing teal, golden eye and bufflehead ducks, some swans, and twelve coot. Paul's decorative work included decoy lamps, miniatures, and natural unpainted decoys in cedar and walnut. Some of the most sought-after decoys are the rare preeners and sleepers he made.

One of my favorite on-going orders for Paul was for one dozen coot. Our friend Henry would write to Paul and include an order for a dozen coot. Paul would write back and say, "Henry, I don't make coot." After many repetitions, Henry tired of the job and turned it over to me. For years, Paul gave me the same answer, but he finally tired of my persistence and said he would think about it. One bright autumnal Saturday morning in 1983, I stopped by the shop to see if Paul had anything for me. As I called out for Paul I heard him upstairs in the shop. When I walked into the paint room, Paul said, "Get these coot out of here before someone else sees them and orders a bunch." It was the only order that I ever picked up from Paul that he tossed out of the second floor to me on the ground, announcing his intentions by saying, "Can you catch a duck, boy?"

A decoy shop becomes a special place for a collector and a lover of decoy history. Such was the case with Paul Gibson's shop. There I was in a historic shop listening to tales of the good old days from someone who had lived them. Paul left a monumental gift to carving when he died in 1985.

Collecting Decoys in Harford County

I PURCHASED a pair of canvasbacks at an auction in Cecil County in 1974. They were clean, well painted, and a good-looking pair of decoys. At the time I thought they were McGaws or Hollys; all that I knew for sure was that they were from Havre de Grace and they were branded "J Pusey." I was driven to find out who J. Pusey was and who had made these birds. I started with the phone book and found one John Pusey near Aberdeen. I called the number one evening after 8 o'clock and wakened Mrs. Pusey. She told me to call back the next morning at 11, their lunchtime. Following her instructions, I made the call and set up an appointment to show Mr. Pusey the decoys on the following Saturday morning at 7. The reason for the early visit was simple: they got up by 5:00 a.m. and were in bed before 8:00 p.m., had lunch at 11:00 and supper at 4:00. Over the next twenty-seven plus years, I was to learn well that schedule. John M. Michael Pusey, son of Joel Pusey, shot each morning at daybreak; he shot the "crow blacks" (grackles) that flew out of the marshes of Aberdeen Proving Ground just at sunrise to feed in the corn or bean fields on the Pusey farm. I watched him shoot many mornings—perpendicular shots, directly overhead it appeared to me, a difficult shot, but one at which he was highly proficient. He shot two Winchesters, both pump actions, one a Model 12 and the other a Model 97. His retriever, Dash, would go after the downed birds and bring them back to an area behind John's pickup truck. For me, someone with little exposure to a trained retriever, watching Dash was a fascinating experience. John spoke not one word, but Dash would watch for the birds and return with them one by one, appearing to arrange them in some type of order, one beside the next, all in a row. When I inquired about the overhead shots, John told me that he had learned to shoot in his father's sinkbox before he turned fifteen; the gunner's supine position in the sinkbox limited one to overhead shots. It was an easy shot for him and always done the same way, waiting for the birds to fly directly overhead.

The pair of decoys that I brought for him to see on my first visit were from his father's once extensive rig, which had numbered in the hundreds. His father or grandfather had had the pair of canvasbacks made in Havre de Grace by Captain Jim Holly years before John was born. They had been used by the Puseys for many seasons before being retired to the family's warehouse and then later restored by family friend and decoy carver, Robert McGaw, in Havre de Grace, and given away as presents by Joel Pusey. The restoration of the decoys had been completed in a fashion that I have seen many times. It consisted of removing the decoy's original head and replacing it with a new head, lightly sanding the wonderful old original paint and applying a bright new fresh coat of paint, and removing the lead or iron ballast weight to allow the decoy to sit flat on a shelf instead of rocking back and forth. The finished product was an attractive one, but the historic value of the old gunning decoy was greatly diminished by the

Canvasback drake by James T. Holly, circa 1890, re-headed and painted by Robert F. McGaw, Jr., circa 1940. This decoy, branded "J. Pusey," was purchased along with a hen at an auction in Cecil County in 1974. It was through this decoy that my association with J. M. M. Pusey began.

The Pusey brothers with Dash in the pickup

The Pusey brothers and Dash after a pretty good morning

Snapping turtles from Swan Creek

"restoration." On that first visit, an instant bonding occurred and a lasting friendship was formed. I had found someone who was willing to share great stories of what waterfowling once was, and John Pusey had found someone who was excited to hear what he had to say.

From that first trip, I was to gain an insight into someone who had grown up in a time and place that most can only dream about. John Pusey never climbed into his truck without two essential pieces of equipment, his shotgun and his constant companion, Dash. As I was to find out, there had been many Dashes over the years; it was really the only name that ever worked for one of his dogs. John didn't leave the farm unless it was an absolute necessity. He shot every day of his life as best as I could determine. He was one terrific shot, as good as his double cousin, J. Calvin Michael, who had won Maryland State Trap Shooting events many times. John just preferred to shoot on the farm and not at the range.

The Pusey farm is located adjacent to the Aberdeen Proving Ground and Swan Creek. John Pusey's grandfather, John M. Michael, a leader in the corn canning business in Harford County, had purchased the farm. Across Swan Creek lies Oakington, which was purchased by John M. Michael and his brother, William O. Michael, for $10,000 in 1883. The Oakington farm fronts directly on the Chesapeake Bay. The two properties were truly a waterfowler's paradise. When John Michael sold Oakington to Commodore Richards of the New York Yacht Club, the Michaels and Puseys retained gunning rights on the property. The family had constructed a bridge over Swan Creek, which provided access to both farms. The waterfront ran along the Bay and out to the point, then up Swan Creek. The family had Bay frontage and frontage on both sides of Swan Creek. In the center of Swan Creek, between the farms, lies Maids Island. John told me of hearing about the negotiations between his grandfather and Mr. E. M. Noel and Mr. S. G. Israel when the island was sold. Noel was the owner of the sloop yacht *Susquehanna* and shot ducks on the Flats every season. The island was ultimately sold for $300.

Knowing of my interest in the history and the decoys, John would bring out one or two on each of my visits. They seemed to be everywhere: a Holly teal was resting on a shelf in the old canning house, a pile of Madison Mitchell cork black ducks and small-bodied Canada goose decoys were in the corner of the tractor shed, and a Barnes black duck that had started life as a canvasback sat on the counter in the old store building. The store was literally a store, where the canning house workers could purchase provisions. Sitting on the counter were coffee tins filled with Indian arrowheads that John, his father, and his grandfather had collected. The date and location of where and when they were found were penned on each one. John's childhood marbles were stored in a shirt collar box. Tobacco, pipes, and cartons of cigarette papers were visible on the shelves. A case of Pikesville Rye whiskey sat under the stairway next to unopened boxes of Gold Dust Twin soap powder. A Winchester shotgun advertising sign was nailed to the stairway next to a price list for provisions dated

1926. Decoys were piled under the stairs, and lining the stairs to the loft were unopened wooden cases of Winchester Nublack shotgun shells.

The huge warehouse and the area behind the store counter were always off limits to anyone but John. If a decoy stored in the warehouse was up for sale or discussion, John would retrieve it from the warehouse and put it in his pickup or set it on the ground just outside the locked warehouse door. One day a group of seven Charles Nelson Barnard high-heads were lined up in a row outside the warehouse door—a beautiful sight. I asked John one day how many decoys had been in his rig. His answer was vague, but the suggestion that there had been 300 to 400 seemed to remain a constant.

When John heard that a pair of his Barnard high-head canvasbacks had been sold at a local auction, he raised the issue of what a decoy like that would be worth to me. My response must have revealed my excitement over the possibility that there existed another pair in hiding somewhere. On my next trip to the farm, sure enough, there they were, in all of their regal splendor, covered with fifty years' worth of dust and dirt. Now, instead of floating on the Susquehanna as tollers in front of the Pusey sink-box, they were riding around the farm in a Ford pickup; however, in spite of their current predicament, they still appeared dignified. They came home with me that day and stirred up a bit of excitement among my decoy collector friends. On the next trip, John produced a page from the family's photo album, featuring a Baltimore *Sun* article from November 17, 1929. It included a photo of John. On the album page his mother had written: "John M. Michael Pusey. This was John's first time in a sink box, and although only 14 yrs. he bagged his limit." Resting on the wing on

The Pusey family with Swan Creek in the background

either side of the box was a high-head canvasback by Barnard. That was a good day but so were all of the trips to the farm.

Not every trip to the Pusey farm was for decoys; some were lesson days, when John would attempt to sharpen my shooting skills. Shooting alongside one of the best and one of the last genuine old-time duck men made me a bit nervous. In the store one day, among the piles of papers, I discovered a little leather-bound journal. It was his father's gunning log for 1925. It began, "Nov. 2 1925 Weather thick, rain at 9am ducks killed 60." A few years later I found John's gunning accounts for 1928–29 and 1930–31. He kept the little journals in his truck and would take them out from time to time. He would show me entries in them as we sat in the truck with Dash on cold or wet days or, on warm days, on the steps leading into the storehouse.

After I had made dozens of visits to the farm and many decoys had left with me, I talked my way into the warehouse. There were no lights at all in the warehouse, just the sunlight from one open door as I stepped down onto the board walk in front of the shotgun shell loading area; down I went in an instant—the boards were covered with hundreds of lead shot pellets. I had just discovered John's security system; the pieces of shot on the floor made normal walking next to impossible. The obstacles got worse—boat anchors and ropes, iron and lead decoy anchors with attached strings, boat oars and poles, and the occasional decoy, all sticking out just about every place that I could see in the dark building. The smell of gunpowder, dust, and dirt from the earthen floor filled my head. The venture inside was always brief, as John would position himself between the good stuff and me, saying, "There is really nothing much in here" or "There is nothing that I want to sell right now—maybe another day when it's a little warmer."

So it went for many visits. We would sit on the tailgate of the pickup and I would listen to how it used to be and why there were no good ducks on the Flats. "Some of those young boys in Havre de Grace, you know the ones I mean. Why they would kill the last canvasback on the Flats then brag on it; you know, no one respects anything or anyone these days." I kept going back. I would help him out with some of the bureaucrats in the county seat when he needed a building permit, and we would talk.

On the first day of spring in 1991, I had taken along enough cash to buy one good duck if the opportunity came up, but instead I made the same offer for a walk to the back of the warehouse. *It worked!* In we went, John and I, stepping over and walking around the accumulation of a huge canning operation, a farm, several households, and a lifetime on the water. When we reached an area about twenty feet from the back of the building, I was instructed to stand still. John lifted the edge of a canvas tarpaulin and pulled it back, and there before me were piled the largest group of duck decoys I had ever seen, all waiting for me. The next sound I heard echoes in my head to this day; it was a horrible, unforgettable noise, one that I had never heard and that I hope I never will again. For access and visibility, John was standing on top of the decoys, walking on them and dragging the tarp to the side of the building. I know that the sounds were not loud, but with each step I swear I could hear a body crack, a neck break, a bill snap off. I pleaded for him to stop, that we could move the tarpaulin together, systematically. "Don't be silly—this won't hurt them at all. How do you think we used to handle them, with kid gloves?"

The relationship changed that day. My newly acquired access to that pile of decoys and that much history increased the frequency of my visits. I was even allowed to take my son on a tour of the warehouse, an opportunity that he will cherish as much as I have. Over the years, in addition to admiring and acquiring decoys, I discovered and purchased gunning lights, bailing scoops hand carved by Blacksmith Charley, push poles for a skiff, block or loom oars and sculling oars for the bushwhack boat, john ducks for the sinkbox, cast-iron sinkbox decoys, and hundreds of cast-iron anchors for decoys.

One day, a canvasback drake by Robert F. McGaw was waiting for me when I arrived; it was mint, perfect, and quickly recognized by me as a mate to the McGaws that were illustrated in Barber's *Wild Fowl Decoys*. McGaw had presented a pair to Barber on a trip to Havre de Grace in 1929. This decoy was from that same group; John's father had purchased all but that pair from McGaw that same year. They had gunned over many of them but surprisingly had stored about a dozen in the attic. I always found this interesting, since the Puseys generally treated decoys as tools. They seem to have made an effort to hide these away for the future. These decoys were among the best of Bob McGaw's total production and the very best canvasbacks he ever made. They are slightly undersize, have the most precise painting, and the necks are attached to a portion of the body which is elevated, creating a shelf, unlike any other decoys by him.

Several visits later, on the morning of December 18, 1993, John permitted my son and me to enter the warehouse just after daylight. Although the morning was cold, the dealing that ensued warmed me thoroughly. In a matter of about ten minutes of discussion, to my surprise, John had agreed to let me buy all the decoys on the floor of the building. We started carrying the decoys out in bushel baskets, about six or seven to a basket. For the first half-dozen trips, John filled the baskets and my son and I carried them the length of the building through the maze that seemed to become more cluttered with each trip. Then, on one of the trips from the warehouse, I heard a noise behind me and turned. There was just enough light beaming through the door for me to see John grabbing decoys as fast as he could and dumping them into an oxcart that sat just to the right of the pile. I realized he just couldn't let go of so many at once. These wooden things had been a part of his life for over sixty-five years, and now they would be leaving the farm for good. Today I'm sure that I would have done the same as he did; I just hope the day I may face the choice is a long time away. I got 100 decoys that day. Among my favorites are the branded ones, not just the "J.P." and "J.Pusey" brands, but also

The store of Clarence C. Pusey on Union Avenue in Havre de Grace. Mr. Pusey bought and sold wild ducks from his establishment in the 1890s.

those bearing the brands of the *Twilight* and the *Reckless,* gunning scows of the Susquehanna Flats, "P&M" for Polhemus and Moore, who owned the *Reckless,* and "RSDFC" for Charles Raymond of the San Domingo Farm Club. These old decoys had lived an entire life prior to joining forces with the Pusey rig.

I kept a record of every trip to the farm; there were 113 trips total and all together 300 to 400 decoys, just as John had said. Looking back over the years and trips, the decoys and the stuff, I cherish them all. They can never be replaced, so I relive them. I look at the decoys and know that for each one of them there is another story.

Branded Decoys

M Y FIRST DECOY had the letter *H* carved in front of the ballast weight, an insignificant feature to a young boy, but an unanswered mystery that deserved further study. The carver of that first decoy was also unknown to me at the time, but years later I was to recognize the style of Benjamin Dye of Perryville. Thirty years after I received my first decoy, I found one of its rigmates—made by the same carver and with the same letter *H* carved in the identical location. In an interview with Nelson Heisler McCall of Charlestown, Maryland, I discovered that the decoys that belonged to McCall's grandfather, Captain Joseph Heisler, a guide from Charlestown, wore that brand.

A certain allure is involved in the act of collecting; this unknown force causes people to accumulate stuff, to acquire things. Some collectors want to acquire every example of what they collect, while some want to gather what they consider the best. Some collect because they consider the items good investments; others desire them for their beauty. A few simply love the collected objects for the history they contain or the stories they left behind.

Decoy collectors desire to know the provenance of the birds on their shelves—who made them, where they were made, where they were used, and who used them. The key to the mystery of many Chesapeake Bay decoys is best found in the brands that were burned or carved into them. Brands were necessary to keep order among the enormous rigs that floated on the Bay, and because of these brands historians are able to trace the history of the decoys that wear them. These branded decoys are the true tellers of tales. By learning the history of the brands, collectors are able to travel through their imaginations to the origins of their decoys.

To many serious collectors, the provenance of a decoy is as important as the paint and condition. For Chesapeake Bay collectors, brands establish the ultimate provenance. Brands were used on the Bay as a form of insurance by the owners of large rigs of decoys, both by market hunters and sport gunners. Decoys often drifted from the rig, at the will of winds and tides; sometimes they were led astray by an overenthusiastic decoy gatherer. The brands represented an individual's name or initials, a gunning club, or the name of one of the gunning scows that served the many sportsmen who traveled into the area for the gunning season.

For many decoy collectors, the only thrill better than finding a branded Chesapeake Bay decoy is tracing the history of the brand. For years, some wonderful Holly and Dye decoys with inletted iron pads wearing the initials T.J.H. and E.L.B. eluded positive identification of ownership. The experience of uncovering the mystery of those brands and identifying them as belonging to the rigs of Thomas J. Hayward and Edward L. Bartlett was as satisfying to me as discovering an entire rig of decoys. A decoy with an unidentified brand can be as puzzling and intriguing as a decoy whose maker is unknown.

Many Bay decoy brands have been identified, and they are listed below. However, the identities of the brands of hundreds of historic decoys remain unknown. The pursuit of this knowledge keeps dedicated decoy historians constantly alert for new information. Over thirty years ago, an early mentor and teacher related to me, a young assessor with Harford County, that by the time I thought I knew the business I would suddenly realize how little I really knew. So it often seems with the serious student of decoys. By acknowledging that we have only scratched the surface, by sharing knowledge and reliable historic facts, we can continue this relentless quest with a measure of success. And the discovery of each additional clue provides a flood of satisfaction.

LIST OF IDENTIFIED DECOY BRANDS

(The brands are listed in a narrative sequence.)

T.J.H. Thomas J. Hayward, a partner in the iron foundry business of Bartlett and Hayward, used a cast-iron pad with his raised initials to mark his decoys. There were over 500 decoys in the rig in 1896.

E.L.B. Edward L. Bartlett and his partner, Hayward, cast their iron pad weights at their foundry in Baltimore. They gunned at various sites in Harford County, owning four farms on the Bush River.

J. PUSEY Joel Pusey of Swan Creek, Maryland, left his brand on a large number of Susquehanna Flats decoys in his 500-bird rig, which included several Charles Nelson Barnard high-neck canvasbacks.

J. Pusey's brand from Swan Creek, Harford County. Lee Mitchell, Pusey's cousin, painted on his initials in 1934.

J.P. This is another brand used on the Pusey rig. It has not been determined which brand was used first; perhaps they were interchangeable. The brand has been found on some Barnards but more often on Robert F. McGaw canvasbacks.

P.K. BARNES Perry K. Barnes was a Cecil County, Maryland, gunner with an extensive rig. His brand surfaces from time to time.

R.K.B. The initials of Richard K. Barnes of Charlestown, Cecil County. Several decoys carved by William Heverin have been found wearing this brand.

PHILADELPHIA DUCKING CLUB This club bought a 144-acre farm at King's Creek on the Bush River in 1851. In 1896, they listed 300 decoy ducks in the club's inventory. Most decoys were branded "Philadelphia Ducking Club"; others read "Philadelphia Gunning Club."

C.A. POST This brand belonged to a New York gunner whose family was among the original owners of the Spesutia Island Rod and Gun Club. All of the known decoys with this brand were originally used as wing ducks on a sinkbox.

CARROLL'S ISLAND One of the most famous gunning clubs on the Gunpowder River in Baltimore County, it was located directly across the river from the Cadwalader Farm. The Carroll's Island Ducking Club held the pedigree for Chesapeake Bay retrievers for over 100 years.

R. M. VANDIVER In a famous Susquehanna Flats photograph, Robert Vandiver, a wealthy gunner from Havre de Grace, is pictured sitting in a sinkbox surrounded by more than 300 decoys.

J. GRAHAM John Graham, an undertaker and decoy maker from Charlestown, Maryland, used this as his personal brand.

N.P.W. The brand of Nelson Price Whitaker, the owner of a substantial iron foundry at Principio Furnace, Cecil County. He gunned exclusively from a sinkbox rig on the Susquehanna River.

SPESUTIA I. R&G CLUB The Spesutia Island Rod and Gun Club, one of the most famous clubs in Harford County, purchased their first gunning shores, on Spesutia Island near Havre de Grace, in 1889. Membership was reserved for the very wealthy; J. Pierpont Morgan was a later member of the club.

RSDFC The brand of the San Domingo Farm Club. The *R* is for Charles Raymond, president of the club. This club, from Oyster Bay, Long Island, leased shores on the Gunpowder River in Harford County in 1883 from

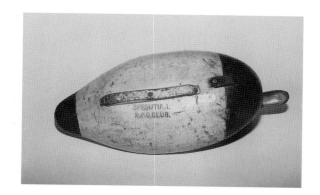

Spesutia Island Rod and Gun Club's brand

The brand of Charles Raymond of the San Domingo Farm Club on the Gunpowder Neck

John Cadwalader, who owned over 7,000 acres on Gunpowder Neck. In 1896, the club listed 500 decoys and six swans in its inventory.

WITUW The brand of the gunning scow *Wituw* from the Susquehanna Flats, circa 1890.

NORTH CAROLINA The name of another gunning scow from the Susquehanna Flats, also circa 1890.

TWILIGHT A rare brand, again for the rig of a Susquehanna Flats gunning scow circa 1890.

W.W. The brand of Wilson Whitlock, it has surfaced on only a few choice Ben Dye decoys, particularly the Dye ruddies. Whitlock, possibly a partner of Dye, gunned over a sinkbox rig on the Flats. It was also the brand of William Williams, a member of the Marshy Point Ducking Club in 1854.

GRACE The brand of either the gunning scow *Grace* or the Grace's Quarter Gunning Club.

W.P. For Winward Prescott. It appears on one of the few known preening decoys made by John Graham.

P & M This brand identifies the decoys from the rig of Henry D. Polhemus and William E. Moore. Polhemus was the owner of the gunning sloop *Reckless,* of Havre de Grace, and Moore was her captain.

G.B.G. / D.G. ELLIOT George Bird Grinnell and Daniel G. Elliot were early outdoor writers and sport gunners. Their brands appear together on Holly decoys with a rare inletted strip lead weight.

CANVASBACK The brand and name of a Susquehanna Flats gunning scow, it appears primarily on the bottom of John "Daddy" Holly decoys.

E. PEARSON Edwin Pearson of Havre de Grace branded those decoys used in his personal rig, whether made by him or purchased.

SUSQUEHANNA A brand derived from the name of a sloop owned by E. M. Noel of Baltimore City.

RECKLESS A brand, along with P&M, used on the rig of the scow owned by Henry D. Polhemus and captained by Billy Moore.

J.D. MALLORY Mallory was the son-in-law of Edward L. Bartlett and member of the Board of Governors of the Chesapeake Bay Dog Club.

C.H.G.C. The brand worn by the rig of the Charter Hall Gun Club located near Perryville in Cecil County.

R.F. MCGAW McGaw branded the decoys that he made for his own personal use.

A.H. TAYLOR This brand appears on decoys carved in Charlestown by John Graham. Either Taylor or Graham added glass eyes to each of these decoys.

G.C.C. The brand of the Gunston Cove Club on the Potomac River. Many examples wearing this brand are cork canvasbacks in the style of Samuel T. Barnes.

F.S. For Frank Sullivan, who was treasurer of the Marshy Point Ducking Club.

J. SUMMERILL & B. This brand appears on Graham and Dye decoys from Cecil County. The identity of J. Summerill and B. is not known.

J.D. POPLAR Poplar had an extensive rig and worked in the shop of James T. Holly.

WIDGEON For a gunning scow of that name from Havre de Grace. This brand appears on decoys carved by the Hollys.

F. TOWNER Another brand seen on Holly decoys. The Towners owned a gunning lodge on the Bush River Neck in Harford County known as Towner's Cove.

S.Y. TECH The brand from the rig of the steam yacht *Tech,* owned by the DuPont family.

J. COUDON The brand of the rig of Joseph Coudon of Aiken, Maryland.

G.W.J. The brand of George W. Jackson of Perryville, Cecil County.

W.W. FOULKES Foulkes was a Philadelphia hunter who gunned from a scow on the Susquehanna Flats.

J.S.M. The brand of J. S. Michael of the Oakington estate and also of John S. Mitchell of Aberdeen. Both were in the canning business in Harford County, and both gunned on the Susquehanna Flats.

J.M.M. This is the brand of John M. Michael of Oakington, the father of J. S. Michael.

L. PENNOCK This was the first brand of Lou Pennock, a Cecil County gunner. It appears alongside the ballast weights on a number of Cecil County–carved decoys.

LP Later, Pennock started using this brand. All known examples appear carved in the tails of Heverin decoys.

H.C.W. The brand of Harry C. Weiskittel, the owner of the Marshy Point Gunning Club after 1922.

H The ultimately simple brand of Joseph H. Heisler of Charlestown, Cecil County.

E.R. The brand of Edward Robinson of 217 South Street in Baltimore, who owned a clubhouse on the Gunpowder River.

G.L.M. Glenn L. Martin, a pioneer in the aircraft industry, gunned in Cecil County over a rig that included both Upper Bay and Ward brothers' decoys.

Teal of the Upper Chesapeake

*I*T WAS OCTOBER of 1966 in Newark, Delaware, at the Kiwanis Club Decoy Show when my old friend Henry and I had the opportunity to examine a bushel basket filled with historic Susquehanna Flats teal decoys. The initial viewing was an exciting moment, but upon closer inspection, the decoys proved to be brand new, antiqued copies of the rarest of the rare—teal decoys from the Upper Chesapeake Bay. Although the decoys were precise copies, the technology available in 1966 to age paint was not greatly advanced. In fact, these frauds had probably been painted with latex or acrylic paint, which quickly peeled from the bodies. At that time, few collectors had been exposed to forgeries in the decoy world. In 1934 Joel Barber wrote in his work *Wild Fowl Decoys* that "in addition to Swan decoys another rarity among the host of American stool ducks is the Blue and Green winged Teal." William Mackey lamented in 1965, in his book *American Bird Decoys,* that teal decoys "all too rarely turn up on the Chesapeake." It was revelations such as these that most likely led to fakes invading the antique decoy marketplace. What Chesapeake wildfowler would ever have dreamed that some day greedy forgers would be luring collectors with copies of objects that were once used only to lure the wary fowl?

Thirty-four years later I saw two decoys from that bushel basket surface on an auction table at Crumpton, Maryland. Time and weather had aged the pair sufficiently that they brought respectable prices, high enough that their newly assigned values created the false image that they were legitimate waterfowling artifacts, a sad fact for the decoy world. That early experience and the more recent one have made me ever vigilant in my search for the genuine article. I became determined to find real historic gunning teal. I have searched every antique show, antique shop, boathouse, loft, and shed I could find for old duck decoys. In all those years, and of the thousands of decoys I have located, I have uncovered no more than twenty of the diminutive teal decoys. On the very best of my decoy-hunting days, in 1984, I left the Pusey canning house in Aberdeen, Maryland, with six wonderful blue-wings that had been carved in Havre de Grace in 1929 by Robert F. McGaw. Although exceptional little birds, these decoys are perhaps the newest of the great early Susquehanna Flats teal decoys. Few were ever made, and very few have survived. Many early teal decoys "changed"

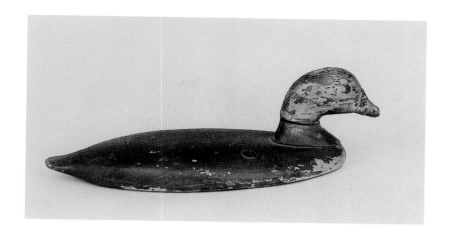

A blue-wing teal by James T. Holly, circa 1880, a rare wooden wing duck

species, and under the paint of a scaup (bluebill) or ruddy duck their true identity hides.

Of the migrant waterfowl, the teal, also called the blue-wing and green-wing, arrive from the North the earliest in the season. They make their first appearance on the Upper Chesapeake in early September. The Baltimore *Sun* of September 14, 1871, reported on its front page that "Blue-Wing Ducks and Reed Birds, Bay Mackerel, Taylors, Trout, Rock, Perch and other Fish" were available for sale at the market of S. R. Scoggins, No. 7 Hollingsworth Street, in Baltimore. In F. C. Kirkwood's *A List of the Birds of Maryland,* the following accounts of the blue-wings' arrival were mentioned: In 1893, "A bunch of 15 were noted in Bear Creek, on August 20," and on September 17, "a bunch of 10 on Loch Raven, in Dulaney's Valley . . . evidently they had just arrived from the north and were tired out." On September 23, 1889, the journal of the *Rough Ashlar* (a gunning scow out of Havre de Grace) reported the following: "Found the scow in pretty good shape and poled over to Carpenter's Point at 10pm. Put out early in the morning in Billy Day's battery box and had very pretty shooting up to 9am————-The wind then went down and the tide fell so the Flats were all bare and had to wave in the scow. Blue wing teal 16, Sprig tail 4, Willet 1, Baldpate 4, Marsh 2, Total 27." Another early mention is recorded in the journal of the Marshy Point Ducking Club, of Baltimore County, on November 8, 1858: in addition to 19 redheads and 2 crow bills, E. A. Oelrichs and Henry Oelrichs shot 2 blue-wings. These early dates of fall arrival are confirmed in the records of the Biological Society of Washington, where in recording migrations for the years 1859 to 1929, they list September 18, 1903, as the earliest fall sighting of green-wing teal and July 25, 1926, for blue-wing teal.

The strongest evidence of the teal's early arrival date lies in the paint pattern used on these decoys. The paint mimics the eclipse phase of the male plumage. The males are slow in molting the female-like colors, which they assume in summer before shedding their wing feathers and becoming temporarily flightless. The blue-wings do not take on full normal body plumage until December, while the drakes of most fowl have attained it by the end of September. Susquehanna Flats teal decoys from the late nineteenth century and early twentieth century that still wear their original paint all appear in the female-like colors.

Teal offered Chesapeake hunters targets from the preseason, through the regular season, and then again on their migration north in the springtime. Reports of teal during the regular season have been recorded in the journals of several gunning clubs. The Eildon Ducking Club, incorporated January 6, 1886, under the laws of the State of New York, owned the gunning scow *Widgeon.* Their Harford County headquarters was Eildon Farm, located adjacent to the Spesutia Narrows. In a journal entry from Saturday, March 20, 1886, the Eildon Club reported that 5 canvasbacks, 2 redheads, 12 blackheads, 1 baldpate, and 1 green-wing teal were shot. On Sunday, April 3, 1887, 19 blackheads, 1 green-wing teal, 1 coot, and 2 hell divers were recorded. From April 21 to April 27, 1888, the *Maxwell's Point Visitors' Book* of the Cadwalader family's estate on the Gunpowder River records that teal were shot. In 1898, on February 18, one teal, a green-wing, was shot at Maxwell's Point. The Carroll's Island Ducking Club *Game Book* shows that on April 1, 1899, 4 redheads, 7 baldpates, 1 black duck, and 1 blue-wing teal were killed. A fifteen-year-old John M. M. Pusey of Aberdeen made the following entry in his *Gunning Account:* April 28, 1930, "two blue-wing teal, 1 snipe." The following years included these references: April 22, 1931, "shot 1 groundhog, 2 blue-wing teal and 1 snipe"; on April 28, 1931, "4 plover and 2 blue-wings"; on November 1, 1931, "2 green-wing teal"; on April 28, 1932, "5 snipe, 2 plover and 1 teal"; and on April 29, 1932, "1 snipe, 4 plover and 1 teal."

Not all decoy carvers from the Upper Chesapeake made teal. Many carvers created only the most popular species—canvasbacks, bluebills, redheads—and occasionally black ducks and mallards. Some of the teal carvings are precise miniatures of full-size decoys. In Havre de Grace, John "Daddy" Holly and his son, James T. Holly, carved beautiful teal. A blue-wing carved by James T. Holly, if held close to a Holly hen pintail, will show his inspiration. Charles T. Wilson, a schoolteacher and public office holder, created some exquisite teal, including a fine example presently in the outstanding Shelburne Museum collection in Shelburne, Vermont. (The Wilson teal that is at Shelburne was found on a shelf in a small storeroom at the rear of Robert McGaw's shop by Joel Barber, as reported in his book *Wild Fowl Decoys.*) Those carvers worked approximately between 1850 and 1920. Following in their tradition, Robert F. McGaw, also of Havre de Grace, carved teal in the 1920s and 1930s. A few examples of James T. Holly's teal have been found in what appears to be original McGaw paint. Cooperation and sharing most certainly existed among early carvers in such tight-knit communities as Havre de Grace.

Across the Susquehanna in Perryville, Benjamin Dye was carving a few teal in the 1850 to 1890 period. A teal by Benjamin Dye closely resembles his redhead decoy. During this same time in Charlestown, on the North

East River in Cecil County, John Black Graham was making some beautiful decoys; he obviously relied on his mallard for the teal decoy pattern. Scott Jackson, also of Charlestown, made a small group of magnificent teal. All of his known teal were discovered in the mid-1960s at an antique show in Baltimore County. Each was painted identically in what can only be described as 1920 Packard deep maroon. In addition to the well-known decoy carvers of the region, some unknown carvers created some beautiful teal decoys. I have one stylish teal, a creation of an unknown carver, that at the proper distance appears to have the exact profile of a black duck decoy by the same carver.

The teal decoys of the Upper Chesapeake are diminutive and very stylish; the longest of them measures a mere 11 ½ inches from the tip of the bill to the tip of the tail. Although some may think of these wonderful little creations as "cute," I would save that term to describe the Susquehanna Flats ruddy duck decoys, which are equally rare.

The early waterfowl histories make little mention of the use of decoys in the taking of these early visitors to our shores. Most teal shooting was done along the shorelines. In his work *The American Sportsman,* published in 1857, Elisha J. Lewis said of these little birds, "They stool better if the decoys are set in the mud than if in the water, and in this respect differ from every other duck. . . . The markets of Philadelphia abound with these ducks, which are sold for a mere trifle. They are considered best by epicures when split open and broiled, with a dressing of butter: we prefer them in this way to all other modes of cooking." Joseph W. Long in his book *American Wild-Fowl Shooting* of 1879 commented on alternative decoys for the shooting of teal: "When shooting teal or mallard in very shallow water with but few decoys, lumps of mud, pieces of bark, or bunches of brush of the proper size may be judiciously employed to deceive the ducks. . . . I have known ducks to decoy all day to a little rough patch of ground left bare by the melting of the ice along the main shore."

I have discovered only three cast-iron sinkbox decoys used for the shooting of teal. These decoys are in the style of Charles T. Wilson. Two of these creations have their heads jutting forward in a swimming position, while the head of one is upright. Each has raised eyes, indicating that the decoy which was to form their mold had carpet tacks for eyes. These birds were found with traces of their original teal paint appearing under the scaup paint. In 1981 in the cellar of a wonderful old house in Aberdeen, Maryland, while examining a rig of decoys with my son, we uncovered the only wooden blue-wing teal wing duck that I have ever seen. The owner of this rig had acquired them from Herbert Barnes, son of Samuel T. Barnes, one of the famous decoy carvers from Havre de Grace. The decoys were stacked under the stairway leading down to the cellar. They were arranged to occupy the least amount of space possible. The bodies were turned in an alternating pattern, one row with the heads turned up, the next with the heads turned downward; across the top, two tightly stretched rubber straps held the entire rig in place. There were canvasbacks and bluebills carved by Barnes, Holly, and Currier and some great-looking decoys by unknown carvers. Directly in the middle of the stack and as if by design to be the centerpiece of the entire arrangement was this tiny little decoy looking directly at me. It proved to be a James T. Holly blue-wing teal wooden wing duck; it had never been altered or rigged for any use except to rest on the wing of the owner's two-man sinkbox. As diminutive as was practical, it measures only 10 inches in length, 1 inch in body thickness, and 4 inches at its widest point.

The early arrival of teal gave eager gunners an opportunity to practice their skills prior to the arrival of the highly sought-after canvasbacks, redheads, and bluebills. The existence of teal decoys for sinkboxes tells us that the sinkbox gunner experienced "darts" of teal. Teal fly in flocks of considerable size, but their maneuvers in the air are truly remarkable. They fly in tight formation and at very high rates of speed, twisting, turning, and banking with miraculous precision. But, being unsuspicious in nature and flying tightly grouped, they become easy targets for skilled shots. Lewis commented, "Blue-winged teal fly with great rapidity and considerable noise; they drop down suddenly among the reeds, much like a woodcock." My good friend from Crisfield, Bobby Tawes, reported that the last dart of teal he had a shot at were flying in groups so close and moving so fast that they reminded him of a "gang of Somerset County mosquitoes."

The early journals report rather modest numbers of teal killed, yet their flocks seemed to decline. *The Proceedings of the Biological Society of Washington,* Volume 42, March 25, 1929, reported the following about green-winged teal: "Formerly a common fall migrant, but now rather rare; casual in winter; very rare or accidental in spring, only two records. Since 1905 it has been recorded in only five years." Of the blue-winged they stated: "Common migrant, less commonly seen on the open river. This has been called a wintering species, but the records do not bear this out; there are no records of its occurrence from the middle of December to the middle of March." Further down the Chesapeake Bay, in Dorchester County, the Bishops Head Fish and Gun Club recorded a total of 1,723 wildfowl killed in their gunning log for the season of 1925–26. Not one teal was among them. Wooden teal are scarce in this region, and it must be the hope of all of us that the live ones have not become scarce at our hands.

A Whiteness of Swans

I WAS IN MY office in Bel Air one day some thirty years ago when I received a call from a friend who had heard on one of those radio "yard sale" shows about some decoys for sale. He thought I might be interested. After obtaining directions, I was on my way to Havre de Grace to check out this lead. It was November, and the ducking season had just opened. I reached my destination earlier than expected, walked up to the front gate, then around the house to the back door as directed by the seller. As I knocked upon the door of the closed-in porch, I could hear a commotion within; minutes passed before a young man opened the door to let me in. He seemed nervous, and both he and the porch were a mess. He had been cleaning the day's ducks, and feathers and buckets of water covered the floor; the freshly picked fowl lay on top of the chest freezer. I was quickly escorted to the cellar to view the rig the young man and his father were selling. They had recently inherited these decoys and were eager to buy new gunning decoys. A variety of species and makers were represented. The duck decoys were $10 each and the full-bodied geese $15. To this day, I can see the one bushel basket with two very different decoys resting on the top. I passed by this group, not recognizing the maker. Years later, I came to the realization that these had been hollow-carved redheads by Charles Nelson Barnard. Much later, I did buy that pair, but at a price for which I could have purchased the entire contents of that basement. On that day thirty years ago, I came away with one high-head Canada goose and four ducks.

As I passed through the kitchen, the cause of the earlier disturbance appeared in my line of vision. I spotted a pair of shiny black webbed feet and the white tail feathers of North America's largest waterfowl showing below a group of hunting coats hung along the wall. I commented to the father that that was certainly a big white duck hanging there and that I didn't realize they were in season. He replied, "Well, you know these boys from Havre de Grace; they have to get that swan thing out of their system early in the season or they think about it every time you take them gunning."

For eons, millions of migratory waterfowl have visited the shores of the Chesapeake. Of all of the species that make their biannual journey through this region, the majestic and noble wild swan is the most easily recognized by even the least knowledgeable of amateur ornithologists. It

This swan from Dorchester County, circa 1915, was constructed with a removable neck and bill for easier transportation and storage.

A 4-gauge breech-loader and two proud Chesapeake Bay retrievers ensured this gunner of a successful day.

has also been described as the most beautiful, most elegant, most graceful, and most spotless of all fowl. There are two varieties of swan that are native to North America: the trumpeter swan and the whistling swan. The trumpeter follows the Pacific Flyway, venturing into the Central Flyway as far as Missouri and Indiana. The whistling swan covers a much broader area of the continent, with about half of their total population wintering on estuaries of the Chesapeake Bay and Currituck Sound. The trumpeter population was almost totally exterminated in our nation's early history. Our European ancestors prized the beautiful pure white feathers and quills. The Hudson Bay Company exported 108,000 swanskins to London, England, between the years 1823 and 1880.

There are few significant physical differences between the two species. The trumpeter is slightly larger, and the whistling has a yellow spot on the bill in front of each eye. The yellow mark is not always present; therefore the only consistent difference in appearance is a salmon red streak on the edge of the mandible of the trumpeter. There is a difference in the calls of the two birds, the trumpeter's being hornlike and the whistling's like a bark-whistle. The male swan is known as a cob and the female a pen. All immature swans are known as cygnets. According to Elisha J. Lewis in *The American Sportsman,* sporting terms describing groups of wildfowl by species included "a flock, team or badelynge of wild ducks; a company or trip of wild ducks; a gaggle or flock of geese; a flock of teal; a gang of brant; and a whiteness of swans."

Swans were once present in great numbers on the Chesapeake Bay. Frank Forester noted in his 1848 *Field Sports of the United States* that the Bay was "a great resort for Swans during the winter, and whilst there they form collections of from one to five hundreds on the flats near the western shores. . . . The connecting streams also present fine feeding grounds. . . . The food they are most partial to is the canvass-back grass—*Valisneria Americana*—worms, insects, and shell-fish." As early as 1844, J. P. Giraud noted that swans were "quite common on the Chesapeake Bay during winter" and that the flesh of the young was "highly esteemed for the table." Lewis described the habits of swans in his book, observing that the swans were "at times . . . quite numerous in the vicinity of Carroll's Island, more particularly if the weather continues boisterous for several days, when they retire from the mid-bay to seek food on the shallows of the coves or under the protection of the islands a considerable distance from the sea." Lewis further noted, "Swans are very shy, fly high, and are not easily brought down unless struck in some vital part. The flesh of the cygnet, or young swan, is considered excellent. We have eaten of it frequently, but cannot say that we have any great predilection in its favor. One thing is certain, however: it is superior to the wild goose, but inferior to the canvas-back." It is recorded in the *Bulletin of the United States National Museum* (no. 26) of 1883 that swans were "frequently exposed for sale in the [Washington, D.C.] market; but such individuals, and those which so

November 21, 1898—a whiteness of swans
illustrated in the Maxwell's Point journal

commonly serve as signs for restaurants during the winter, are probably mostly shot on the Chesapeake, or, at any rate, not in the District."

In 1895, Frank C. Kirkwood in his collection of field notes on Maryland birds said of the whistling swan:

> Common winter resident on the broad waters of tidewater Maryland, and during spring and fall flights liable to be seen anywhere in the state. On September 26 ('93), one was shot on the Potomac near Weverton, by John Leopold. On November 4 ('93), several bunches were at the same place, while on April 15, 16 and 17 ('93), two were on the reservoir at Hagerstown. While swans are more or less difficult to shoot, they often 'bed' on broad water out of range in large numbers. On January 20, 1894, I counted 82 standing on ice at the mouth of Gunpowder River, and a week later 194 on the water at the same place, where I am told they at times appear in greater numbers.

Concerning the trumpeters, Kirkwood remarked, "Casual on the Atlantic Coast. 'In Turnbull's list . . . this species is included on the authority of reliable sportsmen who have shot it on the Chesapeake Bay.' "

Genuine swan decoys are the rarest of all decoys, but swans do take to decoys readily. However, in the minds of sportsmen, the shooting of swans was never really considered equal to duck shooting. When point shooting was practiced in areas such as Maxwell's Point, Bengies, or Carroll's Island, an occasional swan would be taken while the gunners were sitting awaiting a flight of ducks. The Bel Air *Aegis and Intelligencer* of February 1, 1878, noted the following: "Wild ducks are scarce on our waters, but swan and wild geese are said to be more plentiful than usual. Robert B. Taylor, of Gunpowder Neck, killed a swan, last Thursday, which weighed 18 ¼ lbs." The Carroll's Island Club in their record of game killed reported on February 8, 1884, "Mr. Higgins Killed two SWAN flying over the Bar-one falling dead on the Bar, the other falling on the ice in White Oak. John got him by walking on the ice & pushing boat ahead of him." The *Aegis* of December 27, 1889, reported in "Our Bush River Neck Letter" that "scarcely a wild duck can be seen on our waters. The Havre de Grace duck hunters, not satisfied with the shooting line assigned them, are coming down into our waters, and with their rifles have hunted the swan and geese until they too have been driven away." On March 13, 1897, the entry in the Carroll's Island *Game Book* recorded, "Gov. Griggs, Roebling, Latrobe, Marbury, Prof. Rimren [sic]. Great many ducks in Saltpeter. The three swan were killed in Haw Cove at one shot by the Governor of New Jersey . . . about 57 other swan were badly frightened." Percy Thayer Blogg in his work *There Are No Dull Dark Days* described the shooting of swans by the members of the Miller's Island Ducking Club: "There were two 4-gauge guns which belonged to the club and which were used by members for swan and goose shooting, the shells containing 12 drams of black powder and as much number 2 shot as could be crammed into them. It was astonishing to note at what distance 'Big Liz' could pull a swan or goose out of the air." The club owned one of the best-known swan decoy rigs, as Millers Island was a rendezvous for countless numbers of swans.

Swan by Lloyd Tyler, Crisfield, circa 1930

Swan, Upper Chesapeake Bay, circa 1890. This decoy has the paddle tail of Charlestown style and a head and neck reminiscent of James T. Holly's style.

The most significant step towards saving the giant white birds was the Migratory Bird Treaty Act of 1918. This act officially closed the season on most swan shooting. Maryland has never opened a season on swans since then. However, the big white bird proved too tempting a target for many waterfowlers. On April 9, 1932, John M. Pusey of Swan Creek noted, "one swan, one plover, and one crow" in his gunning account. After the Migratory Bird Treaty Act, most swan decoys became a part of decoy rigs as "confidence birds"; hunters, being well aware of the fiercely protective nature of the big white bird, would use them with duck decoys in an attempt to imitate nature.

Swan decoys can be categorized into six distinct groups: the most rare and desirable, which are the gunning decoys made prior to 1918 for swan shooting; those made after 1918 to complement duck hunting rigs; those made for rigs used in body booting on the Susquehanna Flats, to aid in concealing the hunter (the gunner stands in shallow water in the midst of his decoy rig wearing a wet suit; those made since 1930 for use as an integral part of black duck gunning rigs); decorative swan decoys used as "mantle birds"; and the least desirable, those contemporary swan decoys which are created by counterfeiters in an attempt to fool the unknowledgeable collector of antiques.

The construction of proper swan decoys required a huge piece of wood. Some of these decoys weighed from twenty to forty pounds. The height of the neck and size of the decoy required a substantial ballast weight. In the area surrounding the Susquehanna Flats, swan decoys were made with a large attached keel weighted with iron or lead for proper balance in the water. R. Madison Mitchell modified this design to allow for easier storage and transportation by hinging the keel. These became known as "barn door keels." Due to their enormous size, a number of the earlier swans were made of cork or were hollowed out to reduce their weight. Mitchell carved six diving swan decoys to be used exclusively with the small rigs of his black duck decoys. These carvings utilized the full-size swan body but did not include a neck or head. At the breast front, a one-pound mushroom-shaped lead weight was screwed into the body; this would cause the decoy to tip forward, its tail sticking straight up out of the water, mimicking a feeding bird.

The genuine historic swan decoys are as scarce and rare as early teal and ruddy duck decoys. They make a prized addition to any decoy collection. Swan decoys are highly desirable not just to the hard-core decoy collectors but also to the novice or occasional collector. Some examples by James T. Holly and Samuel T. Barnes, both well-known Upper Bay decoy makers, have sold for six-figure sums. The gracefulness of the carving added to the scarcity makes a swan decoy the centerpiece of any collection. The largest rig of swan decoys belonged to the Taylor's Island Ducking and Fishing Club, which encompassed 400 acres of land, including Taylor's Island off the shore of the Bush River Neck and a tract across Romney Creek at Locust Point. Their assessment schedules of 1896 and 1902 valued their 400 duck decoys at $80 and their 20 swan decoys at $12.

A group of five swan decoys, each hollow-carved, was found on the Bush River Neck of Harford County. All can trace their origin to this area. They are masterfully executed and among the finest carved decoys from this region. In 1934, Harry Emmord of Perryman presented his neighbor Oliver P. Boyer with two of these hollow-carved swans. Boyer's farm fronted on the Bush River in the area now named Perryman. The swans most likely were gunned over at the Taylor's Island Ducking and Fishing Company. After the decoys were hollowed, the maker fitted them with white pine bottom-boards that are barely detectable. The necks were attached to a raised shelf with a one-inch dowel. A smaller dowel was attached to the swan's head and fitted into a recess near the top of the neck. Three of these hollow-carved swans have curved necks and two have straight necks. One example is painted a light gray to achieve the look of a cygnet, or immature swan.

The swan decoy has gone from the working environment to the folk art genre. The majesty and mighty presence of North America's largest waterfowl have endured for thousands of years and have captured the imagination of artists of every sort throughout recorded history. An anonymous poet, quoted in Elisha Lewis's *The American Sportsman,* penned this description in 1855:

> The stately-sailing swan
> Gives out his snowy plumage to the gale;
> And, arching proud his neck, with oary feet
> Bears forward fierce, and guards his osier-isle,
> Protective of his young.

Portraits of Carvers

Charles Nelson Barnard

I CAN QUICKLY recall the single decoy auction I consider to be the best I have attended. It was not in Maine, Hyannis Port, or New York City, but in my own home county of Harford. The auction ad said "Perryman, Maryland, July 26–27, 1980, selling antiques, antique guns, and old ducks." It was a hot day on the Bush River at George Gabler's waterfront crab house. Tables filled with a collection of hundreds of salt and pepper shakers sat next to antique oak china closets, large-bore fowling pieces, iron sinkbox decoys (referred to by the auctioneer as door stops), two cast-iron coot decoys, and the largest group of decoys by Charles Nelson Barnard that I had ever seen. Noble canvasbacks, diminutive yet jaunty little bluebills, and a single spectacular black duck branded "Spesutia Island Rod and Gun Club" were on the auction block. The smallest of the bluebills measured a mere 9 inches in length. My lifelong friend and mentor, Henry, was on those Barnards like nothing the huge crowd of auction regulars had ever seen. When the auctioneer had dropped the gavel on the last of the decoys, the few major collectors divvied up the spoils, Bobby Richardson getting a few, Dick McIntyre getting a few, Henry Fleckenstein toting off decoys by the bushel basket, and me, the new kid on the block, walking away with two great little pairs of Barnard bluebills. As it has turned out in the twenty years that have passed since then, I've seen maybe three other bluebills by Barnard, but the best were sold that day.

Charles Nelson's brother, Joseph C. Barnard, was a friend of George Gabler, steamed crabs with him, fished with him, and went ducking over his brother's decoys with him. In the summer, Joe and his wife, Phoebe, lived in front of the Gablers' shore on the Bush River in a skipjack that Joe had converted into a sharpie, a motorized cabin cruiser. During the winter months, Joe and Phoebe lived in the historic Lock House in Havre de Grace.

Charles Nelson Barnard was born in Havre de Grace, Maryland, in 1876. Born into a waterman's family, he sailed and worked the Chesapeake Bay and Susquehanna River on the *Ella Barnard,* the scow belonging to his father, Captain Charles Thomas Barnard. Charles Nelson was taken out of school while in the fifth grade to work on the *Ella Barnard* and vowed as a youngster that he would leave his father's ship upon reaching the age of twenty-one. Shortly after his twenty-first birthday, he moved to

Baltimore City, where the American Can Company employed him. Apparently, city life did not agree with the country boy, as he returned to Singerly, near Elkton, in Cecil County in the late 1890s.

Unlikely as it may seem, this native waterman turned to the rails, as did many of his contemporaries. He went to work for the Baltimore and Ohio Railroad in 1915 and rapidly reached the level of signalman. He retired from this position in 1950. Also in 1915, Barnard moved back to Havre de Grace, purchasing the property at 609 Stokes Street, where he resided until his death in 1958. It was here that Barnard raised his five children—three daughters and two sons—Edna, Emily Marie, Lola, Frederick, and Homer.

There is no documentation verifying when Barnard started to carve. I think that the most accurate date would be a few years prior to the 1915 move to Havre de Grace. This date would answer some of the questions concerning the Barnard style. Beginning to carve on the Cecil County side of the Susquehanna River, he was undoubtedly influenced by some Cecil County carvers. The number of carvings he produced is also subject to conjecture, but most knowledgeable decoy students agree that his production was no more than a thousand pieces. One detail recalled by family members is that of the last major rig he produced. In 1937, he carved 300 decoys for United States senator Millard Tydings. Barnard and Tydings had been friends as young men, and Tydings continued to be a decoy customer and occasional visitor to the Barnard shop.

Charles Nelson Barnard is shown at the center of this photo of signalmen taken on the B&O Railroad near Aiken, Maryland, in 1910. Standing is a Mr. Smallwood, and Charles Botts is seated alongside Barnard on the speeder.

Barnard enjoyed making miniature decoys and produced several different styles and sizes. I have seen one totally unique example of a hollowed-out miniature with a lift-off top. This delightful piece was obviously made as a jewelry box or pocket watch holder. Some of his miniatures measure a mere 1½ inches in length. The Barnard family used many of the miniatures in their Christmas garden, with some resting on a mirror to simulate ducks on the water. Flying miniatures hung from the Christmas tree just over the mirror.

Barnard's decoys follow few of the characteristics of the typical Havre de Grace bird. Each decoy is a hand-chopped creation with a shelf rising from the body to support the head. Unlike most Havre de Grace decoys, there is no rise to the tail. It leaves the body perfectly straight, with a clear, crisp, ridgeline found in the center. The decoys, with a truly paddle-like tail, are like very few Havre de Grace birds. The best-known of Barnard's works are the magnificent high-neck canvasbacks, some with necks reaching nearly 6 inches in height, most of which he made for use by Joel Pusey of Swan Creek. These birds were used as tollers and placed at the front of the rig of decoys surrounding a sinkbox. John M. Michael Pusey, who gunned from a sinkbox with his father, Joel, told me that, depending on wind and other conditions, they would sometimes lead off a sinkbox rig with a pair of tollers some ¾ of a mile away.

An opposing theory on the appropriate use of the high-heads was to place them close to the sinkbox, as a further disguise of the box and hunter. One famous photograph of John Pusey shows him shooting from his sinkbox with a Barnard high-head perched on the box. However they were used, the Barnard birds achieved (better than any) the true look of a canvasback duck. Whether sitting in the water or on a collector's shelf, they are without equal. No one living can attest to the actual number of high-necks produced by Barnard, but sixteen is the generally accepted number. In the *Maryland* magazine of the autumn of 1991, a feature article on Chesapeake decoys said this of the high-necks: "Collectors of Upper Bay decoys consider his high-neck canvasbacks to be the finest example of a working Upper Bay decoy, possessing exquisite form with a simplistic but very serviceable paint pattern." In their Classic Hunting Decoys and Sporting Art exhibit of September 1994 to January 1995, the Ward Museum of Wildfowl Art described Barnard's work by saying, "These distinctive high-necked canvasbacks exemplify his best work."

In addition to these high-neck canvasbacks, Barnard produced ducks with several other neck heights, including one with a very low neck and thin body, which achieves the posture of a contented or resting bird. Barnard also made redheads, bluebills, and black ducks in addition to his canvasback production. Only one example of a Barnard ruddy duck decoy has appeared, and no one known to me has yet to uncover one of his coot decoys. Several examples of his hollow-carved birds exist, a very atypical decoy for Havre de Grace. Barnard's younger son, Homer, remembers clearly the pleasure his father found working on a very novel approach to a hollow-carved decoy. He placed in the cavity a round lead ball. The lead ball was mounted to a small section of steel spring, the idea being that if the water moved the decoy, the ball would bounce against the inside cavity walls with the spring causing a rebound from side to side. This would give the decoy additional motion, achieving a more natural, lifelike action. The whereabouts of this decoy remain a mystery, but five or six examples of hollow-carved black ducks and redheads have surfaced.

Barnard's patterns changed over the years. He produced four very distinctive styles of canvasbacks, the last pattern dated in Barnard's hand "1946," but only one style of redheads and bluebills. The black duck style remained constant as well.

The last full-size decoy carved by Barnard was a hollow-carved canvasback drake. Barnard made this piece with a much different purpose than his working decoys; it was created for his grandson, the late Perry Barnard, in 1950 as a three-year-old's own special decoy. It was hollowed out to weigh less in a young boy's hand and made with glass eyes and extra attention to the paint details. It was his only effort at a full-size decorative carving. It stands as evidence of the durability of his work that after many years of use by a young boy, this object quickly was transformed into a decorative piece on the young man's bookshelves.

Charles Nelson Barnard was not the only member of his family to carve. His older brother, Thomas P. Barnard, who resided on Ontario Street in Havre de Grace, also carved decoys. Thomas's production was apparently much more limited than that of his younger brother. Like Charles he carved miniature decoys. He produced flying canvasbacks with applied metal wings. Thomas died in 1927 after a bout of pneumonia. Charles's oldest son, Frederick T. Barnard, worked in his father's shop as a young man and produced a few hundred decoys during his lifetime. The only species known to have been carved by either Thomas or Fred was the canvasback. Fred Barnard was responsible for introducing Captain Harry Jobes to decoy carving, and Jobes became one of the most prolific of the Havre de Grace carvers.

There has been much discussion among students of Upper Chesapeake Bay decoys concerning which carvers actually worked together or influenced one another. For example, did the Holly family actually produce the enormous quantities of birds that are attributed to them or did others work for the Hollys, much as many young men have worked for Madison Mitchell? Was there a time when Robert McGaw, Paul Gibson, and Madison Mitchell worked together, or was the strong similarity in their carvings simply a matter of influence? It is without question that Charles Nelson Barnard worked single-handedly on the majority of his decoys. However, the family tells with great detail of Charles's exchanging baskets of carved heads and bodies with Thomas. Those decoys attributed solely to Thomas are distinctive in that they have a subtler paddle tail, with barely a hint of a ridge on the tail near its center.

Canvasback drake with medium-height neck, circa 1915

This black duck demonstrates Barnard's skills at re-heading a decoy. It is a Barnard head on a solid body carved by Taylor Boyd of Cecil County. This decoy is branded Spesutia Island Rod and Gun Club and was made circa 1910.

Pair of hollow-carved black ducks with tack eyes, circa 1910

Decoys from the Upper Chesapeake Bay have been described over the years in many terms: graceful, sleek, sturdy, practical, and even stately. Some collectors and enthusiasts from other regions of the country become confused when studying Upper Chesapeake Bay decoys. A few have gone so far as to say that they all look pretty much the same. They frequently ask how we can tell one carver from another. There is always one exception to this, and that exception is Charles Nelson Barnard.

Barnard's work is highly sought after by collectors. His decoys have been displayed at the Ward Museum of Wildfowl Art, the Chesapeake Bay Maritime Museum, and the Havre de Grace Decoy Museum. Examples of his work have now been sold by all of the decoy auction houses, as well as Sotheby's in New York City.

If Upper Bay decoys are stately, Barnard's birds are dignified. If the Susquehanna Flats produced decoys that are sturdy, Barnard produced work that was forthright. If one studies closely the very few photos that exist of Charles Nelson Barnard, the same dignity and pride show in the face of the man that appear in his carvings.

Robert F. McGaw, Jr.

TWENTY-FIVE years ago while visiting a friend in Havre de Grace, I was invited inside his home to look at his decoys. I was admiring several decoys carved by R. Madison Mitchell and Paul Gibson when my friend said, "I want to show you my good decoys." I was distracted and thought "Well, what could be better than Mitchell's and Gibson's"? Robert F. McGaw, the man who had taught those two, had carved the birds he then showed me, two sets of miniature decoys mounted on walnut bases. I was immediately drawn to these delightful little ducks. They were two sets of pairs, one with the normal head position and the other with high-heads. My interest in Bob McGaw decoys was immediately piqued, and the search began.

The McGaw family were living on Spesutia Island by the 1850s. Bob McGaw's grandfather, also Robert F. McGaw, joined with Otho Scott in ownership of that portion of the island known as the Upper Farm. In 1864, McGaw paid Scott $9,000 for his share of that farm. This tract was bordered on the north by the Chesapeake Bay, on the east by a creek called Back Creek, and on the southwest by the Spesutia Narrows. Robert McGaw's son, Robert F. McGaw, Jr., was a canner at Boothby Hill, now a part of the Aberdeen Proving Ground. Robert Sr. died in 1878, and his son, as was the tradition in those days, assumed the title *Senior,* even though he as yet had no son bearing the name. One year later, however, the next Robert F. McGaw was born, on the island, and became Robert Jr. His family operated the ferry between the island and the mainland and they also were the purveyors of supplies for the island. When young Bob enlisted in the Maryland National Guard, where he served in the First Regiment Infantry from 1909 until 1911, he gave his occupation as insurance collector. He attained the rank of corporal and was rated an expert rifleman. It was shortly after his discharge that he began making decoys.

On November 26, 1918, McGaw married Carrie Polhemus Moore. Carrie was the daughter of Captain William E. Moore. The middle name of Polhemus was the surname of the family who owned the gunning scow *Reckless.* Captain Moore piloted the *Reckless,* a famous gunning scow built in Havre de Grace, which carried sport hunters from New York, Philadelphia, and Baltimore to hunt the ducks for which Havre de Grace was so famous. Captain Moore also served as a ducking police officer by appointment of the governor, as did Bob McGaw's father. There is little doubt that Carrie was well suited for the life she led with Bob McGaw.

In 1919, Bob and his wife purchased property at the corner of Washington and Girard Streets in Havre de Grace. At the rear of the lot, Bob built his two decoy shops, facing Girard with Lodge Alley to the west. One structure, used for storing blocks and finished decoys, was referred to by Bob as "The Boar's Nest." The other shop building, heated by a potbellied stove, was used for the production of full-size and miniature decoys. The equipment was powered by an electric motor which was attached to a "jack shaft." This shaft was mounted on the east wall of the shop.

The handsome yet functional decoys of Robert F. McGaw, Jr., are highly sought after by collectors today, but few may realize the historical significance of his carvings. Bob McGaw changed the course of decoy making forever. McGaw's decoys were hand chopped, roughed out on a band saw and then shaped with a hatchet and spoke shave, until he purchased a duplicating lathe in 1929. He was the first carver on the Susquehanna Flats to utilize a lathe to produce decoy bodies. The lathe allowed him to manufacture a consistent body size, shape, and style with speed and efficiency. His lathe was sold to Madison Mitchell and then to Paul Gibson, both carvers of the Havre de Grace style bird. Dozens of Havre de Grace carvers use lathes today to produce thousands of decoys each year.

Bob's decoys were weighted with dog bone–shaped ballasts fastened with a nail, one on each corner and one in the center. His painting reflects the influence of the earlier works of Sam Barnes and the Holly family; one outstanding feature of his paint is the refined scratch-painting technique first used in Havre de Grace by James T. Holly. McGaw used a much finer instrument that produced a very thin feathering style. He is also noted for his strong diagonal wing speculums.

Bob McGaw's decoys are among the most realistic ever to float on the Susquehanna Flats. Many old-time gunners complained that when a crippled bird swam into their rig, they had difficulty distinguishing it from the McGaw decoys. In an interview with R. Madison Mitchell in 1987, Madison and I were discussing the decoys of other carvers from Havre de Grace. I will always remember Madison's telling me with a chuckle, "Old Bob had more decoys shot up than any other maker in town. You see he made them so damn good that the average pair of eyes couldn't tell the difference from a cripple and Bob's decoy." Bob McGaw was a hunter of ducks. He studied the live birds for hundreds of hours from his blind, sinkbox, and bushwhack boat. Perhaps this is the reason for the place of honor he has won among the waterfowl counterfeiters.

Some of the most beautiful specimens of McGaw's work are his miniatures. His cross-necked geese rise above the norm as prime examples of folk art. Their outstretched necks crossed one another. Carrie McGaw refused to allow the cross-necked geese into her home. Madison Mitchell told me this position offended Mrs. McGaw; she interpreted it as a simulation of part of the mating ritual in wildfowl. Although a few decoy

Robert F. McGaw outside his decoy shop with his dog Queenie and a grouping of his decoys

carvers from the Susquehanna Flats produced miniatures prior to McGaw's time, he raised the standard from mere models of working decoys to decorative miniatures when he mounted them on hardwood bases. He attached both miniature and full-size birds to bases and sold thousands of them to early collectors for purely decorative purposes.

The rarest of the decoys carved by Bob McGaw are actually more correctly referred to as diving devices. There are only two known examples of these devices; both are black ducks. One is pictured in J. Evans McKinney's book, *Decoys of the Susquehanna Flats.* Both of the diving black ducks were produced in the 1930s. Only three other decoy makers from Havre de Grace are known ever to have made such decoys. Both Paul Gibson and James Currier also made black duck divers, while R. Madison Mitchell made a diving swan. When these diving devices are compared to each other, it appears as if the makers cooperated on their design and engineering. However, when the McGaw black duck device was shown to Madison Mitchell, not only had he never seen it before, but he did not know that McGaw had made such an item. The McGaw black duck diver appears to be of the same body as the well-known and equally rare McGaw teal. The breast is squared off in the identical fashion as the breast of the Mitchell diving swan. But rather than the mushroom-shaped lead used by Madison Mitchell on his swan, McGaw inserted a one-inch wooden dowel, three inches in length, into the breast and screwed a rectangular lead onto the dowel. On the underside of the body near the breast, a small lead in the style of Paul Gibson's ballasts is attached.

The old-timers around Havre de Grace who knew Bob McGaw often relate tales of his sense of humor. When inspecting his black duck device, one can instantly imagine the moment of whimsy in the McGaw shop

A group of McGaw miniatures

when Bob painted his normal black duck eyes on the rectangular-shaped lead. Sitting among his black duck decoys on the drying rack, the "eyed" lead probably created quite a chuckle for visitors to the shop.

Robert F. McGaw's normal production included the following species in full size: Canada geese, canvasbacks, bluebills, redheads, mallards, black ducks, and pintails. He is also known to have made brants, baldpates, goldeneyes, teal, and the two black duck diving devices. His miniature decoys included swans, Canada geese, canvasbacks, bluebills, redheads, mallards, black ducks, pintails, and a brant or two.

If standards of decoy carving and painting exist for decoys from the Upper Chesapeake Bay, it was Robert F. McGaw who set those standards. Throughout the decoy world, it is accepted that changes in decoy quality and style can aid in pinpointing the stage of a carver's career in which a work was completed. Normally, carving and painting techniques become more precise as a carver develops his skills and then decline through the natural aging process, as the carver becomes less physically dexterous. Some carvers show drastic changes in both their carving and painting skills near the end of their productive years. Robert F. McGaw was an exception to this norm. When decoys he carved in the late 1920s are placed side by side with decoys he produced in the 1940s, even the most critical eyes would be hard pressed to detect the slightest decline in either the carving or the painting skills. Yet Bob McGaw suffered for years from a crippling arthritic condition that greatly impaired the use of his hands. Madison Mitchell often related to me how McGaw had to wrap his paintbrushes with rags in order to properly grip them. I recently placed a 1920s black duck alongside a 1945 black duck. Other than the 1945 model's being slightly larger in size, each is equally detailed and appealing. The very fine scratch painting on his early works does not lose its precise definition on his later birds.

In 1931 New York's Abercrombie and Fitch's famous Log Cabin Sportsman Center displayed decoys by Robert F. McGaw for the first time. Joel Barber's 1934 book *Wild Fowl Decoys* included illustrations of Bob McGaw's canvasback decoy ducks. Barber and McGaw had become friends during the visits that Barber, a renowned collector, made to Havre de Grace. A pair of canvasback decoy ducks, made by McGaw in 1929, were presented to Joel Barber on one of his trips. They were from a rig of twenty-four that McGaw had made for his own use. In 1929, neither McGaw nor Barber could have imagined that the Barber collection would someday form the hub of the foremost collection of decoy ducks in the world, that of the Shelburne Museum in Shelburne, Vermont.

An enormous nationwide mail order business for McGaw decoys was generated by Joel Barber's recognition of them. Another source of buyers was army personnel relocated from the Aberdeen Proving Ground, who had developed a fondness for Chesapeake decoys while they were in the region and continued their patronage from their new postings. Carrie McGaw handled the correspondence and shipping, and Bob kept busy in the

McGaw at work in his shop painting black
ducks in 1929

McGaw goldeneye drake, circa 1930

shop producing decoys as quickly as his one-man shop could turn them out. He also had an active decoy restoration business. His repaints and re-headings can be found on hundreds and hundreds of decoys, including factory-made ones and ones carved by all of the Upper Bay makers. I have personally owned dozens of McGaw restorations and studied them to see if they were restorations or joint efforts by different carvers. Decoys that McGaw restored can fool even the experienced collector. If the decoy had a shelf for the head, the new head would be sized to properly fit the shelf. He did a repaint with the same care he used in painting a new decoy.

On March 22, 1985, the United States Postal Service issued the third in their series of folk art commemorative stamps. These stamps depicted duck decoys of four species: the canvasback, the redhead, the broadbill, and the mallard. A single canvasback decoy duck was selected from the tens of thousands that have been carved over the years. It was a canvasback drake decoy duck made by Robert F. McGaw, Jr., created to float in a decoy rig on the Susquehanna Flats and given to Joel Barber as a token of friendship.

Robert F. McGaw, Jr., changed the method of creating decoys on the Chesapeake Bay forever. His foresight eliminated the hand chopping of decoy bodies, a process which had existed in Havre de Grace since the creation of the very first decoy there. With the use of his duplicating lathe, he was able to create a consistent body shape and size repeatedly. His decoys exhibited excellent form, paint, and a uniformity that had never existed prior to his time.

Samuel Treadway Barnes

*I*N 1924, the Second Annual Exhibition of Wild Fowl Decoys by American Sportsmen was held at the Winchester Sportsman's Headquarters in New York City. The Best in Show award, based on practical use and maintenance of decoys, was given to Samuel T. Barnes, for a pair of his canvasback duck decoys.

In August of 2001, while I was visiting the Havre de Grace Decoy Museum to discuss an ongoing exhibition, a lady arrived with a pair of her grandfather's decoys to donate to the museum. The curator asked me to take a look at the decoys. I have been in a similar situation many times, and the birds usually prove to be awful unknowns, or re-heads at best. When I saw these decoys, I was pleasantly surprised. Not only were they Sam Barnes decoys, but they were the best I had ever seen, a pair of decorative canvasbacks. The donor was Sam Barnes's granddaughter, Dorothy Jaenicke.

The decoys had higher than usual heads that were not so flat on the sides, necks that rested on a shelf approximately ¼ inch in height, tails upswept to a degree like no Barnes decoys I had seen, a carved nail at the tip of their bills, mandibles, and nostrils. They had never been weighted or rigged for gunning, and as I examined them, picking them up and putting them down, they rocked back and forth on the table before me. Had these decoys not been repainted, in the 1940s, they would have been perfect. They said so much about Havre de Grace decoys without making a sound. They were so unlike any Barnes decoys I had previously seen that I was almost to the point of thinking they might be Hollys, when the image of a famous Sam Barnes swan, one of the very few he made, jumped out at me—the tail, the shelf, that elongated body, and the recent debate over whether the swan was a Barnes or a Holly. Holly decoys are typically more refined and stylized than those carved by Barnes. Mrs. Jaenicke pulled out a program from that 1924 decoy exhibition in New York, and, along with it, the blue ribbon prize her grandfather had won for the exact pair of ducks I was handling. Now I somehow felt I knew that swan a lot better— no doubt it was carved by Barnes: If Sam Barnes were going to make only a few swan decoys in his lifetime, wouldn't he carve them a bit fancier than his standard working decoys? If he were going to send only a pair of ducks to an important exhibition in New York, why not finish them with greater

A Samuel T. Barnes canvasback drake, circa 1910

Bluebill drake, cork model by Samuel T. Barnes, circa 1920. The one-inch pine bottom board is evident.

detail than he would when making a gunning rig of 100 or more birds? Surely Barnes didn't anticipate that someday someone would be sitting in a museum (a decoy museum at that) examining his decoys, admiring them, and trying to determine why this pair was different from the last, but he obviously wanted to enter his finest work in the competition.

Samuel Treadway Barnes was born in Havre de Grace, Maryland, on February 20, 1857. In census records and the Havre de Grace city directory, William Ford Barnes, Samuel's father, was listed variously as a carpenter and a "duck shooter." Duck hunting and fishing were vocations for many residents of Havre de Grace at that time, not hobbies or pastimes as in today's world. Such was the case with the Barnes family. Barnes followed in his father's footsteps as a duck hunter and used his own skills with wood and other material to fashion hundreds of practical, utilitarian decoys.

In 1885, Barnes purchased property on Washington Street in Havre de Grace from his father, and he married Sadie K. Gilbert. Samuel and Sadie Barnes were married for forty-one years and reared seven children: four daughters—Isabelle, Florence, Catherine, and Landonia—and three sons

—Herbert, Samuel and Robert. He lived in and worked from the Washington Street property until his death in 1926. In 1896, his 40-by-125-foot lot and the dwelling located there were valued at $910. His personal property at the time was valued at $250—$100 attributable to household furniture and $150 attributable to boats, nets, and ducking outfit. The word *outfit* was the county assessor's terminology for duck decoys and related accoutrements.

The substance of all Barnes decoys is best summarized by the criterion used to judge the decoys in that 1924 competition, practical use. The practicality and strength of these decoys are proven in the number of examples that have survived. Collectors can still find canvasbacks as well as blackheads, redheads, black ducks, and Canada geese. The most famous of all Barnes decoys are the swans he carved in 1890. These decoys probably have been displayed and photographed more than any other decoys in the world.

In September 1931, a few years after Barnes's death, the famous Havre de Grace wild swan carved by Barnes was exhibited in the Log Cabin Gallery of Abercrombie and Fitch at Madison Avenue and 45th Street in New York City. The exhibition was entitled American Wild Fowl Decoys and included old decoys from the collection of Joel Barber and modern decoys by Charles "Shang" Wheeler. In August 1932, that same swan first appeared in print, in an article in *Fortune* magazine. Authored by Barber, a New York architect, it was the first article published on decoys as folk art. The September 1934 issue of the *Sportsman* ran the largest photograph ever published of the Barnes swan.

The provenance of this decoy is related in Barber's book, *Wild Fowl Decoys*, published in 1934. Barber acquired the swan in Havre de Grace in the late 1920s from Bennett Keen, a retired gunner. When Barber discovered it, it was ornamenting the side yard of an old white house on Washington Street in Havre de Grace, in front of a grape arbor. Robert F. McGaw, as-

Canvasback drake, decorative model, 1924. This decoy, which won a blue ribbon at a Wild Fowl Decoy Exhibition in New York, shows the upswept tail characteristic of the Havre de Grace style.

sisted Barber in shipping the swan by rail express to New York. Bennett Keen's Havre de Grace property was situated almost equidistant between Samuel Barnes's and James T. Holly's properties. (I have recently seen another swan decoy with a Barnes-style head resting on a Madison Mitchell swan body. The owner told me that the head was found in McGaw's shop and that McGaw had received it as a gift from Barnes.)

In 1987 the provenance of the swan decoy was discussed again. A mate to Barber's swan was sold at the Richard Oliver auction in Kennebunk, Maine. The sale price of $66,000 attests to its value to collectors. A discussion concerning the maker ensued at the sale. Some present thought James T. Holly had made the swan. There are similarities between the work of these two Havre de Grace decoy makers. A likeness in the bluntness of the tails in certain species is strong. Likewise a similarity exists in the base of the neck between some of Holly's work and the swan. Holly did make a few swan decoys, but they differ from the Barnes style of swan sufficiently that experts feel confident in attributing those others to Holly. Having seen the Barnes canvasback pair, I do not question that Samuel Barnes carved each of the three swans that have been attributed to him.

Each of these swans has a Roman numeral stamped on the neck shelf and on the underside of the neck. This suggests that they were made about the same time. Barber's swan resides at the Shelburne Museum in Vermont. A second rests on a shelf in the Chesapeake Bay Maritime Museum in St. Michael's, Maryland. The third, sold at Oliver's 1987 auction, is now in a private collection.

In addition to his wooden decoys, Barnes is credited with being the first Susquehanna Flats carver to use cork for decoy bodies. Cork examples include canvasbacks, redheads, blackheads, and black ducks. A one-inch white pine bottom-board was attached to the work with four screws. A threaded screw runs through the head, attached by a nut countersunk into the bottom board. A flat piece of lead, approximately 1 inch wide, 4 inches long, and ¼ inch thick, fastened with a nail at each end was used for ballast.

In a September 1992 interview with the late R. Madison Mitchell, he told me that all of Barnes's cork decoys were made prior to Mitchell's association with him in the late 1920s. (After Barnes's death in 1926, Mitchell filled the outstanding orders for wood decoys.) The idea of using cork was inspired by some Long Island cork decoys. Many gunners on the Susquehanna Flats also gunned in New York and traveled back and forth as the fowl migrated. Mitchell recounted that a Joseph Gilbert, who resided on Washington Street next to the Barnes family and worked as a refrigeration technician at Aberdeen Proving Ground, where cork was used extensively for insulation, brought them surplus cork. Since the Proving Ground did not open until 1918, this places the creation of Barnes's cork decoys at the end of his career as a carver. Except for the dust created in carving it, cork was easier to work with and certainly easier and lighter to handle. Many of these cork decoys have survived, some in original paint.

The usual lead ballast weight on Barnes decoys is very similar to the weight later used by another local carver, Paul Gibson. This is not surprising, since Gibson made his first decoy, a miniature canvasback, in Barnes's shop. This wonderful little decoy appears to be in original Barnes paint. The heads on Barnes decoys are much flatter on the sides than are those by most Upper Bay carvers. Some collectors refer to them as "board heads," although close examination reveals a slight flair on each side of the head behind the bill.

Barnes decoys are also blockier than most decoys, especially those produced by the Holly family. Although there is an upswept tail, it does not rise to the height of the tails of most Havre de Grace decoys. One rare Barnes blackhead is made from a 3-inch block with a 1½-inch-thick wooden keel running the length of the body. His usual lead ballast is attached midway to the keel. Many of the original-condition Barnes decoys have a tiny ring and staple attached to the under breast for applying the anchor line.

A few Barnes redheads and blackheads have surfaced in original Barnes paint; they have original heads carved by Taylor Boyd of nearby Cecil County. It is not known how this occurred, perhaps Barnes and Boyd worked together or perhaps Barnes obtained the heads from Taylor Boyd. There are some decoys that bear a strong resemblance to Sam Barnes decoys but have plain features and much less style than the typical Barnes decoys, and they are generally attributed to his son Herbert. I have a pristine pair of miniature canvasbacks, which came directly from Barnes's son Sam. The younger Sam carved miniatures in the style of his father's decoys in the late 1930s and 1940s.

Many decoy collectors display their birds to enjoy each and every day. As I walk by my birds, I admire them, handle them, study them, and consider why I appreciate each for its different merits. When I look at my Barnards, I consider their aristocratic, regal form; with the Hollys, it's their smooth, refined, and stylized characteristics. When I look at the decoys of Samuel Treadway Barnes, I see their sturdy, functional form; I consider how well they have survived over the years; and I recall that Best in Show award long ago in New York. Their practical, utilitarian, and functional design has helped them endure, so that now they can be cherished among collectors as fine trophies of American folk art.

The Hollys of Havre de Grace

THE STYLE of decoys carved along the shores of the Susquehanna Flats differs from the styles created in other regions of the country. Most Flats decoys are full-bodied, round-bottomed birds obviously designed to ride well and right themselves in the water in all varieties of weather conditions. The predominant species created there were canvasbacks, bluebills, and redheads. As time evolved, two distinct carving styles emerged in the region, one on the Harford County side of the Flats and the other on the Cecil County side. The Harford County, or Havre de Grace, style is best described as having an upswept tail with no defined shelf for the neck to rest upon. The Cecil County style, or North East River style as it is also known, is quickly recognized by the paddle tail emerging straight from the rear of the decoy and a distinct shelf upon which the neck rests.

The earliest examples of the Havre de Grace style are attributed to John Holly, best known in the decoy world as "Daddy" Holly. John Holly was born in 1818 and died in 1892. Although research does not reveal the exact date that Holly arrived in Havre de Grace, Krider's *Sporting Anecdotes* of 1853 lists John Holly as one of the most highly respected duck hunters from Havre de Grace. Coincidentally, the day that Krider visited Havre de Grace to shoot ducks, John Holly had one of his better days and killed 183 canvasbacks.

Many professional watermen lived year-round on their boats. This could have been the case with John Holly, given that he owned two vessels large enough to provide living accommodations. His will, dated 1880 and filed in the Harford County Court records, reveals that he owned the *William W. Hopkins,* a boat, and the *Jumbo,* a sloop. His name appears in the Maryland census of 1850 along with that of his wife, Amanda, and two sons; his occupation is listed as "carpenter." The total value of his property at that time, as determined by the Harford County assessor, was $200. In the 1860 census, Daddy Holly's occupation is recorded as "fisherman," and four children are listed as living with him—William, born in 1847; James T., born in 1849; John W., Jr., born in 1851; and a daughter, Amanda, born in 1853. Twenty years later the census shows that two of his sons, John W., Jr., and William, were still living with their father, who continued to report his occupation as "fisherman."

In 1866, Daddy Holly purchased a home on Alliance Street at the corner of Lodge Alley. His son John Jr. eventually moved next door. Daddy Holly left his home to William, and the two brothers lived out their lives in neighboring houses as bachelors. The third brother, James, lived two blocks away on Market Street with his wife and two daughters.

The Hollys produced huge rigs of decoys for use by market hunters, local residents, individual sport gunners, and the numerous gunning clubs of the Upper Chesapeake Bay. Holly decoys, wearing the brands of gunners from Long Island to the Carolinas, are found in well-known collections today. The high demand for Holly decoys led to a style of carving that accomplished the desired form more quickly than had their earlier style, by eliminating the unnecessary shelf and paddle tail. Some of Daddy Holly's earliest work exhibited a shelf and well-defined tail, but few examples of it survive. It was surely early in his carving that he eliminated both. As contemporary carvers can attest, the sleek, racy lines of a Holly bird are more easily and quickly shaped than are those of their counterparts from across the Flats. In addition to decoys, the Holly family made gunning boats and sinkboxes and created waterfowl art from the mid-1800s until the 1920s. The decoys that have survived attest to the quality of their creations. The beauty of their birds is recognized throughout the decoy world, with most major collections having at least a few Holly birds. Of all the decoys from the Upper Bay, many collectors consider the Holly pintails, mallards, and black ducks to be the raciest. These species, in addition to the Canada geese and teal, frequently exhibited the precise scratch-painting technique. The development of that technique is attributed to James Holly. It is a technique that requires the scratching of the top layer of paint, while it is still wet, with a sharp pointed device, thus revealing the lighter color of the primer coat. The scratching is done in a fashion to mimic the feathers of the duck.

Canvasback drake with wooden keel, made by John "Daddy" Holly circa 1860

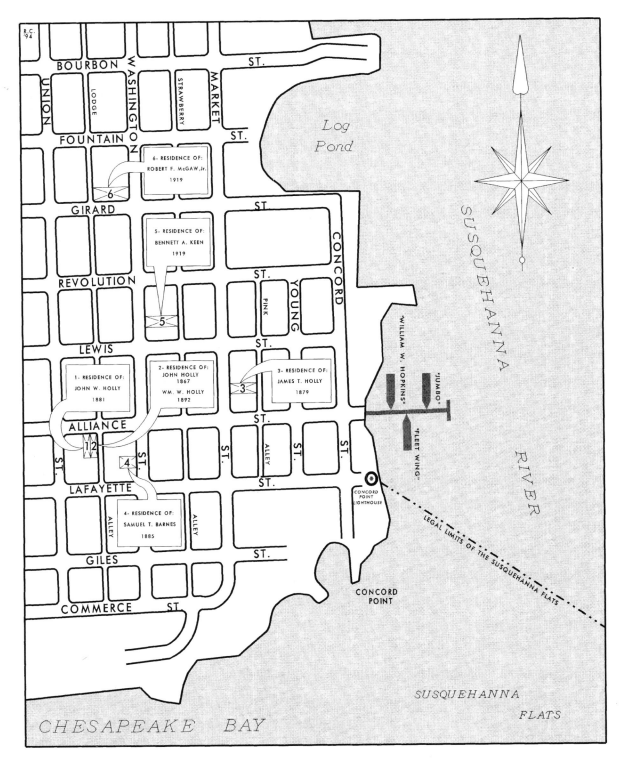

Map of Havre de Grace showing location of the Holly residences, as well as the residences of Robert F. McGaw, Jr., Samuel T. Barnes, and Bennett A. Keen. Drawn by Roger J. Colburn.

The Hollys' sleek looking decoys became the standard for quality, beauty, and style. Their style was adopted by other Havre de Grace carvers. It was from Holly birds that, in 1924, Robert F. McGaw created patterns to fit the first duplicating lathe used for decoy carving in Havre de Grace. These patterns changed little over the years as they were used in the decoy shops of R. Madison Mitchell and Paul Gibson; to this day carvers working in Havre de Grace use these patterns. A lathe pattern sold at the Paul Gibson estate auction in the 1980s was fashioned from an early Daddy Holly body. A slice of wood had been attached around the shelf and under the tail to smooth the contours for duplicating purposes. The old body is in canvasback paint, while the added wood is a clear white pine. These alterations allow one to closely view the original shelf and tail regions. Today the new generation of Havre de Grace decoy carvers continues to produce thousands of decoys each year. Each of these sleek, upswept-tail waterfowl is a tribute to John Holly and his sons, who first conceived this style over one hundred fifty years ago.

Over the years, many theories for identifying a Holly decoy developed. Various styles of Hollys were assigned to the different family members. Those birds with cast-iron ballasts have always been attributed to Daddy Holly. But ballast material and style do not always ensure positive identification. Many years ago, I purchased a group of Madison Mitchell high-head pintails, each weighted with the flat dog bone–shaped sheet lead ballast of Robert F. McGaw, Jr. When I showed one of these birds to Madison and inquired about the ballast, he took me to a corner of his shop and quickly produced a bucket filled with the McGaw ballast weights. They had come directly from Bob's shop when his decoy making days were over. One would expect that there would be an overlap in the use of the iron ballast between Daddy Holly's production and that of his sons. The redhead decoys made by the father for Thomas J. Hayward for the famous Bartlett and Hayward rig were weighted with cast-iron ballast weights made in the foundry of Bartlett and Hayward and carry Hayward's initials, T.J.H. Several Holly decoys in collections have inletted lead ballast weights. These appear in elongated rectangular configurations and in circular configurations. Holly decoys that are highly refined and of the sleekest style have been credited to James T. Holly. Holly birds with broader tails and chunkier body types have been attributed to either John Jr. or William.

Interviews with family members and the old-timers from the Susquehanna Flats have not clarified the proper assignments of the various styles to specific family members. Family members recalled that James T. Holly did in fact learn his decoy carving skills from his father. Verification that John Jr. and William were decoy carvers is in short supply. William is listed as an hourly employee in James Holly's ledger, and they almost certainly helped to complete some of his decoys. Given that John Jr. and William lived with their father as adults makes it hard to imagine that they did not participate in his decoy production to some degree, whether by carving, sawing, sanding, or painting, but the best evidence is that these brothers were associated with the wallpapering and painting trades. When John Jr. died in 1927, his personal property was valued at $113.15. This included everything left to him by his brother William. A part of this sum included tools and brushes used in the painting and wallpapering business. Nothing was included in the inventory that would lead one to believe that the two brothers had ever engaged in any other pursuits. James T. Holly, on the other hand, was clearly an accomplished artist and decoy carver. Unfortunately, those who could verify facts and separate them from fiction now reside in Havre de Grace's Angel Hill cemetery.

Many duck hunters (with the exception of the wealthy sports) carved their own rigs in the Holly years, but the literally thousands of decoys by unidentified makers from the Susquehanna Flats no doubt include unrecognized creations of well-known carvers—perhaps earlier styles, changes in style or mood, or blocks of wood of unusual size or shape; as some contemporary carvers have told me, "some wood just carves differently." The chances run high that some of the unknowns include examples by the Holly family.

In addition to the decoy business, James T. Holly had a highly successful boat and sinkbox building business. He was credited in his obituary with designing the coffin-shaped sinkbox. He was an accomplished, although self-taught, artist, and his illustrations of duck shooting on the Susquehanna Flats are the best-known pieces of art from Havre de Grace. Only three pieces of Holly's artwork are known to have survived; two versions of the duck shooting illustration and a painting of a Havre de Grace ship under full sail are in the possession of Holly family members. He also painted two wonderful signs that I have in my own collection. They say "Private No Thoroughfare" and guarded the bridge over Swan Creek at Oakington. The ledger of Joel B. Pusey reveals that Pusey paid Captain James T. Holly, on June 25, 1918, the sum of $15 for the two signs.

In 1884, James T. Holly was listed in the court records along with a Thomas Healy as ducking police for the Harford County side of the Susquehanna Flats. James, as well as Samuel T. Barnes, Benjamin Dye, and Robert F. McGaw, were all ducking police who were also active in the production of decoys.

Of all the historical decoy-related artifacts available, one of the most important pieces of decoy history is a ledger belonging to James T. Holly. It lists boats and sinkboxes produced by him from 1886 through 1917. It also lists employees who worked along with him in each of his enterprises. The ledger provides a glimpse into the level of his production and the size of his operation. The excerpts printed at the end of this chapter are of special interest to followers of decoy history. The names of those buying boats and sinkboxes are a virtual who's who of gunners from the Susquehanna Flats; included are the 1886 and 1892 purchases by his brother William of two bushwhack boats. The employees in James Holly's shop, who included Ed-

Top: Canvasback drake by James T. Holly, circa
1890. *Middle:* Mallard drake by James T. Holly,
circa 1890. *Bottom:* Mallard hen by James T.
Holly, circa 1890.

win Pearson and Jess Poplar, created decoys for their own use as well as for others. Proof as to how cast-iron decoys were sold is provided in the entry indicating that Admiral Richards bought 240 pounds of iron decoys at 7¢ per pound. In 1901, Holly's ledger reveals, his production to date was 25 sinkboxes and 197 bushwhack boats.

When decoy collecting first attracted nationwide attention and collectors' reference books first appeared on the market, some Holly decoys were attributed to a nonexistent family member referred to as Ben. This was probably an early misnomer for John "Daddy" Holly, confusing him with Ben Dye of Perryville, in Cecil County. In an attempt to correct this situation, a possible overreaction occurred, and positive identifications were assigned to practically all Holly decoys. Now it appears that this trend has subsided, and a quick look through the past several year's catalogs from the decoy auction houses will reveal very few references to any Holly family members except John Sr. and James T. I have always felt that the safest and most honest approach in referring to any Holly decoy is as a "Holly family" decoy since many hundreds of Holly decoys wear paint and/or heads created by Daddy Holly's sons.

Regardless of which family member actually made each individual decoy, the fact remains that the Hollys produced thousands of wonderful decoys. When we admire the Holly style, form, or paint, we are admiring a major part of decoy history. As with the work of great artists, none of the Hollys could likely comprehend the value that collectors now assign to their work.

EXCERPTS FROM THE LEDGER OF JAMES T. HOLLY

Fall of 1886

Wm. Holly	one boat	30.00
Henry Preston	one boat	30.00
Bengie's Ducking Club		

Bluebill drake by John "Daddy" Holly, circa 1870, with head by James T. Holly. My grandparents gave me this decoy for my thirteenth birthday.

Spring of 1887
    Wm. Moore   one boat   33.00
    Fred Moore   one boat   30.00

Spring of 1888
    Middleton   two boxes   14.00

Fall of 1888
    J. Keen   one boat   30.00
    Jess Poplar   one boat   26.00

Fall of 1889
    Wm. Heavern   one boat   30.00
    Barnes   one boat   31.00

Fall of 1892
    Wm. Holly   one boat   25.00
    Perry Barnes   one boat   31.00
    Geo. Wash. Barnes   one boat   30.00

Year of 1893
    Scot Jackson   one boat   32.00
    Walter Jackson   one boat   31.00
    Charles R. Flint   one boat
                fitted out   38.00
    Wm. B. Hurst   box   45.00
    Mickel Andrews   double box
                second hand   48.00
    Sumerill   one boat   32.00

Year of 1894
    Jno. Poplar   one boat   30.00
    Lockard   one boat   30.00
    Jno. Simpers   one boat   30.00
    Charles R. Flint   one double
                second hand box   40.00
                one single
                sink box   45.00

Year of 1895
    Perry Barnes   one boat   30.00
    Jess Poplar   one boat   30.00
    Benny Keen   one boat   30.00

Year of 1896
    P.K. Barnes   one boat   30.00
    H. Simpers   one boat   25.00
    Harry Moore   one boat   30.00

Year of 1898
  Charles R. Flint   one single box   45.00
  Wm. Heavern   one single box   45.00

Year of 1899
  Bartlett & Hayward   two boats   64.00

Year of 1901
  25 boxes, one hundred and 97 boats

Year of 1902
  H. Jeffers   one boat   35.00
  Scow Lilly   one boat   32.00

Year of 1903
  Capt. Heisler   one boat   38.00
  Jess Poplar   one boat   38.00

Year of 1908
  Barnard   one boat   40.00

October 1916
  Admiral Richards   one sinkbox complete   75.00
                          100 Decoy Ducks   50.00
                          240 lbs. iron decoys 7 cts   16.80
                          string & stringing 100 decoys 3.00
                          100 anchors for decoys   7.00
                          60 lbs. iron decoys 6 cts   3.60

Hourly Employees
  Edward Chesney
  Kemp Richardson
  Jess Poplar
  Ed Pearson
  Ramsey Keen
  William Holly

The Grahams of Charlestown

MUCH OF the history of decoy carving is passed along orally. How does one accurately attribute the many styles of a single decoy maker? Unless patterns, descriptions, or actual photographs exist, the process is complicated. The signing of decoys did not begin until the first collector felt that it was important to establish an accurate attribution. We now know the importance of Joel Barber's recording of Charles T. Wilson as the maker of the teal decoys presented to him by Robert F. McGaw. I immediately recognized the significance of attribution when I discovered the head patterns for James T. Holly's decoys; the heir to McGaw's estate had discovered the signed and dated Holly patterns during the emptying out of McGaw's shop in 1958. When a single maker executed various styles, assigning credit to that maker for particular decoys becomes complicated. Who is to say that the decoy makers of earlier days did not employ helpers in their shops, much as is done today? These apprentices could have changed styles and patterns out of personal preference or to simply ease the repetitive task of carving. Accurately assigning credit to a decoy maker becomes even more difficult when entire families were engaged in the business. In the case of the Graham family, decoy production spanned not just decades but several generations.

The earliest record of the Graham family in Maryland appears in the first census of the United States in 1790, in which William Graham appears as a resident of Charlestown. Charlestown had been laid out and developed as a town by an act of Assembly in 1742, "there being as yet no such place settled at or near the head of the Chesapeake Bay," and George Washington recorded visits to Charlestown in his diary on August 10 and September 9, 1795.

The Cecil County tax list of 1786 reveals that William Graham owned property in the "Village of Charlestown" with a total value of $25. By 1795, the value of his holdings had grown to $50, including a 3-acre lot. In 1845, Zachariah B. Graham, William's son, had accumulated property worth $1,642. Business in the Graham family obviously was prospering. By 1867 Zachariah's son, John Black Graham, held property with a total value of $2,353.

John Black Graham was born in Charlestown in 1822, one of twelve children born of Zachariah and Rebecca Lewis Graham. Like his father and grandfather before him, he became a cabinetmaker and undertaker. At the death of Zachariah, Graham took over his father's business and expanded it to include the sale of sand, coal, and fish, as well as boat building and duck decoy carving. During the Civil War, he held the office of county tax collector for Cecil County.

John B. Graham was one of several major decoy makers from the Cecil County area. The others were Benjamin Dye (1821–1896), W. Scott Jackson (1852–1929), William Y. Heverin (1863–1951), George Washington "Wash" Barnes (1861–1915), Henry Lockard (1868–1944), and Carroll Cleveland "Wally" Algard (1883–1959). Early in Maryland's history, Charlestown, which is at the point where the North East River flows into the upper region of the Chesapeake Bay, was in competition with Baltimore as the leading port city of the Upper Chesapeake Bay. As history relates, Baltimore established itself as the major port, and Charlestown became a major site of duck hunting and prolific decoy producing. By 1871, Charlestown was listed in the *Maryland State Gazette Merchants and Farmers Directory* merely as a post village on the Philadelphia, Wilmington and Baltimore Railroad about 43 minutes from Baltimore City.

A unique carving style evolved in this area adjacent to the Susquehanna Flats. In general, decoys from the Flats have round, fat bottoms, balanced with ballast weights, to make them float realistically and right themselves in rough water. The earliest decoys produced on the Cecil County side of the Susquehanna exhibit a paddle tail and a distinct shelf on which the decoy's neck is attached. John B. Graham is generally considered to be the originator of this style of decoys. Although Holly initially made decoys with the distinct shelf and paddle tail that are associated with Cecil County, his style quickly developed into something very different.

For speed in carving, many years prior to the advent of the duplicating lathe, Holly must have reached the conclusion that he could spoke shave bodies more efficiently without the shelf and tail. Along with the elimina-

Canvasback drake with deep wooden keel designed to ride on rough water, circa 1870

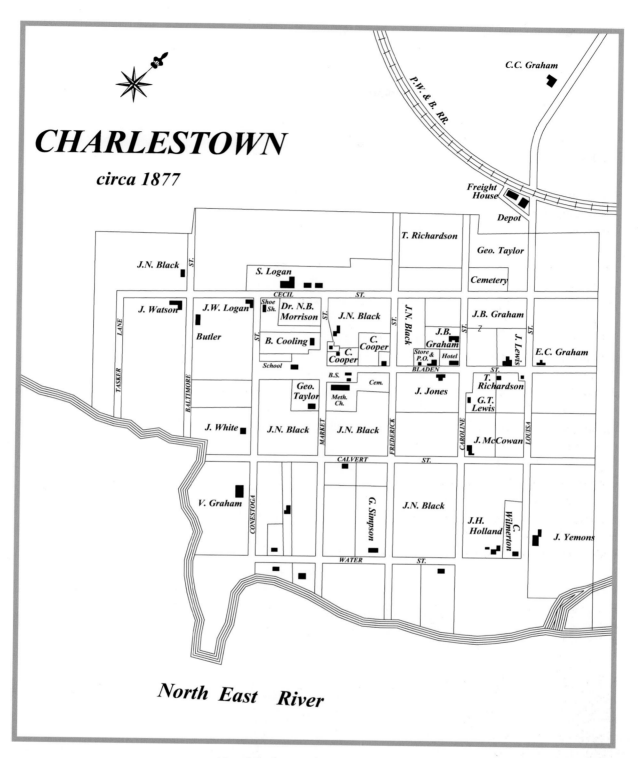

CHARLESTOWN

circa 1877

P.W. & B. RR.

C.C. Graham

Freight House

Depot

T. Richardson

Geo. Taylor

J.N. Black

S. Logan

Cemetery

CECIL ST.

ST.

J. Watson

J.W. Logan

Shoe Sh.

Dr. N.B. Morrison

J.N. Black

J.N. Black

J.B. Graham

Butler

B. Cooling

C. Cooper

J.B. Graham

J. Lewis

E.C. Graham

School

C. Cooper

Store & P.O.

Hotel

Z

BLADEN

B.S.

Cem.

J. Jones

T. Richardson

Geo. Taylor

Meth. Ch.

G.T. Lewis

J. White

J.N. Black

J.N. Black

J. McCowan

MARKET

FREDERICK

CAROLINE

LOUISA

CALVERT

ST.

V. Graham

CONESTOGA

G. Simpson

J.N. Black

J.H. Holland

C. Wilmerton

J. Yemons

BALTIMORE

TASKER LANE

WATER

ST.

North East River

Map of Charlestown showing location of residences of Grahams. Drawn by Roger J. Colburn.

Canvasback hen from the rig of A. H. Taylor

Diminutive bluebill drake measuring eight inches in length, circa 1880

tion of the shelf, the paddle tail was changed to an upswept design. This change likely occurred early in Holly's carving career, early enough that it set the standard design for the Havre de Grace school of carving. The only three known holdouts or exceptions on the Havre de Grace side of the river were Charles Nelson Barnard, his brother Thomas, and Joseph E. Dye. All of their decoys exhibit well-defined shelves and tails.

The Graham decoys from Cecil County always exhibit the shelf and a well-rounded tail. The tail is subtler than on most Cecil County decoys and does not protrude as far from the body as many do. The decoys attributed to John B. Graham encompass many different styles, all close enough in characteristics to be identified as probably his but varied enough to raise some questions. Some variations are minor, such as those of tail length, tail shape, slope of forehead, width of head, slope of bill (Roman nose), fatness of body, and presence of carved mandibles. Other variations are not so understated, such as the replacement of a solid body with a hollow-carved one for black ducks. In addition to black ducks, John B. Graham carved canvasbacks, redheads, bluebills, and teal.

John B. Graham was recognized primarily as a cabinetmaker and boat builder, as is evidenced by the numerous references to him in publications. In 1871, his listing in the *State Gazette* indicated his principal occupation as cabinetmaker. In the *Delaware State and Peninsula Directory* of 1882, his occupation is shown as an undertaker, while his son, John Cooper Graham, appears as a cabinetmaker.

Given the many stylistic variations that appear on Graham decoys, is it reasonable to conclude that more than one Graham made decoys? It is certainly possible that John B. Graham made both solid and hollow-bodied decoys, but perhaps it was his son John who decided that hollowed versions were better for the black ducks and carved them himself. To carry the hypothesis of multiple Graham carvers an additional step, let us first acknowledge that handmade wooden decoys were in use on the Susquehanna Flats by very early in the nineteenth century. Is it not plausible that, if John B. Graham followed in the footsteps of his father and grandfather as undertaker, cabinetmaker, and boat builder, an earlier Graham might well have been the originator of the Cecil County style, as manifested in the so-called Cleveland canvasbacks (reported to have been gunned over by Grover Cleveland), which some consider to be the earliest Susquehanna Flats decoys?

The comprehensive work *Portrait and Biographical Record of Harford and Cecil Counties, Maryland,* written and published in 1897, says this about John B. Graham: "It is worthy of special mention that on the site where he now engages in business, members of his family have followed the same occupation for 120 years, a record perhaps unequaled by any other family in Cecil County." It would be a logical conclusion that the business referred to included decoy making. The *Portrait* continues: "In the possession of John Black Graham were the tools of cabinet making used by his father and grandfather, but they are so different from those now in vogue that the cabinet makers of today cannot tell for what they should be used." We sometimes forget that technical advances existed prior to the twentieth century.

Canvasback, the earliest style of Graham decoy, circa 1860. The ballast weight is fashioned from an iron horseshoe.

Certain advances in the development and design of various types of saws could well have led to minor changes in construction that resulted in subtle decoy style changes over a period of years.

The population of Charlestown in 1882 was 250. It was a close-knit community of families all living on or within sight of the North East River. The *Delaware State and Peninsula Directory* of 1882 lists only eight specialty professions in the town. Three are filled by Grahams—John B., his son John C., and John B.'s brother, F. D. Lafayette Graham, all listed as cabinetmakers and undertakers.

In those days, generations of families were born, lived, and died in the same village, on the same street, even in the same house. Grandfathers, fathers, sons, and brothers worked in the same shop. The Grahams lived together, hunted together, built boats together, made caskets and furniture together, and, most certainly, made decoys together. It is inconceivable that John B. Graham was the only Graham making decoys in Charlestown, Maryland. The variety of styles evident in Graham decoys combined with the listed professions of generations of this family strongly suggests that the diversity evolved from one generation to the next.

The Crisfield Carvers

I N SEPTEMBER 1993, the first Decoy, Oyster Collectibles, and Game Call Auction conducted by Richard W. Oliver took place at the Ward Museum of Wildfowl Art in Salisbury, Maryland. After the annual July decoy auctions in Maine, I joined my old friend Henry Fleckenstein in writing some descriptions for the catalog of the Ward Museum. I made several trips to Salisbury to work in the museum, studying decoys, commenting on their style and overall condition, and entering preauction estimates of value. That summer seemed to fly by, and the auction was upon us just as the cataloging process had begun to run smoothly. The day of September 30 was to be the first day of a buy, swap, and sell event, an antique and flea market for decoy collectors. Dealers and collectors at such events offer decoys and anything remotely associated with them for sale or for trade. Although the event was scheduled to begin at 1:00 p.m., most dealers were on site by 7:00 a.m. This is probably driven by the "early bird getting the best decoys" mindset.

I arrived early, like the rest of the crowd, and headed for the tent where the good stuff was awaiting. Immediately upon entering the tent, I spotted some great-looking early Crisfield flicker decoys; yellow-shafted flickers are large migratory woodpeckers averaging about 10 ½ inches in overall length. The genuine "gunning" birds of this species are now scarce. About the only place flicker decoys were ever used was Somerset County, Maryland. The table before me held several, plus a large variety of carved songbirds and duck decoys, all well carved and looking to wear considerable age. The vendor was pleasant and offered up wonderful stories about each of the birds. His strong accent lay somewhere between North Carolina and Smith Island, Maryland. I've heard Smith Islanders, and their speech reportedly resembles the language of our early English settlers. Some have said that the earliest inhabitants of the island arrived with Captain John Smith when he explored the Chesapeake. These accents require the listener's undivided attention. The tone of this man's voice in combination with his powerful accent, as he told his stories with a twinkling eye and a cigarette dangling from his lower lip, caught me off guard, pulled me in, and held me as would a magnet. It turned out that I was speaking with one of the premier Crisfield carvers, William Zachary Ward, called Bill Zack, or sometimes just Zack. When Zack had finished talking, I owned everything that he had made for the buy, swap, and sell. After that deal was consummated, Zack headed back to Crisfield to carve some more "old birds" that same night.

As the years have passed, Zack, his carvings, and his stories have drawn me back, as they have some other enthusiasts I know. I've been to his house on Byrdtown Road, his "shop," and his trailer. I have met the entire family, and he has met most of mine. He has taken me around Somerset County—"carried me about," as he says. He speaks of the old ways and the old days, and he still lives them. He has introduced me to his vocabulary and his glossary of bird names: the "wadjett" (his name for common merganser), the "wopp" or "bumcutties" (bittern), the "sleepy brothers" or "iron heads" (ruddy ducks), the "flock ducks" (scaup), the "snous" (hooded mergansers), and the "dippers" (buffleheads). He told me of how his mother had traded the long legs of bittern that he had shot in the marshes for real chicken legs to the "uptowners" in Crisfield. She apparently convinced them that they just raised bigger chickens on Byrdtown Road.

One day, during an in-depth discussion of flicker decoy use and the techniques used in Somerset County to "harvest" the migrant woodpeckers, he told me one of the best tales I've ever heard. I mentioned to him that recently, in an old Baltimore *Sun,* I had found an ad for flickers. Flickers, like terrapin, were once available in the Baltimore markets. Zack took off describing in great detail the method used around Crisfield for harvesting the woodpeckers. A "scrag," or small dead cedar tree, from the marshes would be cut and carried to a live tree. Zack would then climb the live tree, hoist the "scrag" up, and tie it in place. The "scrag" would be tied at an angle, creating a limb that jutted out at the top of the live tree. One flicker decoy would be fastened midway up the dead limb above the normal tree line. Zack claimed that after the first northwest wind in November, the flickers would come in flocks that, like those of the migrant blackbirds, seem to fly the way schools of fish swim. Into this darting flock he would shoot box after box of shells with his Remington automatic. He then sold the birds or gave them to hungry friends and neighbors. They found that the tasty birds mimicked the flavor of quail.

When that story was complete, and just as the diamondback terrapin harvesting story was being introduced, I inquired when this flicker hunting had taken place. "In the '60s," Zack replied. "When?" I asked again. "In the '60s—about 1963, 'cause I was out of school for good by then." "Zack," I said, "the ad in the Sunpapers was from the 1850s, not the 1950s." "Well, you know, it takes a while for the news to get this far. And we never did pay much attention to the law. Did I ever tell you about the time my grandfather tried to sell a mess of 'yellow legs' to the game warden in Crisfield, you know he pleaded insanity and was in and out in no time, now how's your mother doing, tell her I was asking for her, and if you ever carry her down this way, I'll have my daughter fix her up a mess of that rockfish and potatoes. Now, let me show you this here Sterling flicker that I just bought off a widow woman in Crisfield, it's a good one, I'm a telling you,

Lem Ward in his shop, August 1983

Goldeneye pair by Lem and Steve Ward, 1936 style

but you got to promise you won't tell no one where you got it." Robert J. Brugger, in his book *Maryland: A Middle Temperament,* accurately described Crisfield as "the closest thing the East had to a Dodge City or Abilene"; he might well have been referring to some of Zack's forebears.

Zack told me that there "weren't but six families in all of Crisfield" when he was growing up: the Sterlings, the Tylers, the Lawsons, the Wards, the Tawes, and the Joneses. His "distant" cousins Lemuel and Steve Ward, Noah and Lloyd Sterling, and the others never thought of selling a

My first Wards, bluebill ducks with balsa bodies and finely carved cedar heads

decoy until they came upon the realization that the Upper Bay carvers were selling entire rigs of decoys to the clubs farther down the Bay. He also spoke of the African-American carvers Pied Jones and his son Sherman, living in what the native Somerset Countians called "Freedom Town." Zack expressed his concern for the young, non-carving generation of Crisfielders; he said that all they do on weekends is drive around the traffic circle—they "drive down the dual-highway that leads nowhere but over-board, going 'round that circle till they wear the left sides off their tires. . . . There's none of them that like to shoot ducks, let alone carve them."

Decoys from the Lower Chesapeake were generally carved after the turn of the century. The earliest ones date just after 1900. The decoys from this region were all carved with flat bottoms, wide hips, and narrow breasts. These solid-bodied "blocks" or "stools" are somewhat oversized. If intended for use on the open water around Crisfield, they have wooden keels attached to their bottoms, with a ballast weight of lead to keep them floating upright. Some of the best-looking and most highly valued decoys were created in the Lower Bay region. The carvings of the Ward brothers, Lemuel and Steve, are considered by many to be the very best. The Ward brothers' ability to blend and apply paints was without equal. They learned to carve at the side of their father, L. Travis Ward, Sr., who was a waterman, decoy carver, and barber. The style of the Crisfield decoys is very different from that of decoys from the upper and middle regions of the Bay. The flat-bottom design allowed a multitude of attitudes and head positions to be created. By turning the head ever so slightly to one side or the other, a different feel is given to the carving. Tucking the head, by shortening the neck, produces yet another attitude.

Prior to the turn of the century, the many carvers of the Upper Bay region filled the demand for decoys up and down the Bay. The smaller demand in the Lower Bay and the flat-bottomed design of that area's decoys allowed the Ward brothers to take their creativity to another level of artistic accomplishment. Their father's decoys had been carved for his own use and the use of a few others from the Crisfield area. However, the reputation of Lem and Steve spread throughout the Chesapeake region, and they produced decoys for gunners in the Upper Bay as well. A few of the gunning clubs ordered Ward decoys, and in some cases a particular Ward style became associated with a specific club. One example is the Canada goose model carved for the Bishops Head Gun Club of Dorchester County.

The Sterling family also produced decoys. The carvings of Noah Sterling were produced at the same time Travis Ward was carving. The best Sterlings, usually attributed to Lloyd Sterling, are at times mistaken for Wards. Lloyd's carving style was so similar to that of the Wards that many experts cannot attribute some pieces to either of them with certainty. Another Crisfield carver of considerable renown is Lloyd Tyler. Tyler lived directly across the street from the Wards, and his carving was greatly influenced by them. His carvings are generally cruder and not as well finished, but they still have much appeal. They tend to be more "folky" and, in their lack of refinement, more unique. To many collectors they epitomize folk art, and they attract as much attention as some of the more refined Crisfield carvings. Tyler never painted the bottom of a decoy and bragged on it, saying it was nothing but a waste of time and paint.

In 1974 I purchased my first decoys by the Ward brothers, two bluebill drakes. They were balsa models carved in 1948. The Wards purchased surplus life rafts after World War II and used the balsa for decoys for years. I remember my first impression of those decoys—highly refined, well-carved heads on very plain bodies. In 1979 I purchased a pair of great-looking Ward canvasbacks, oversize and obviously made for what they referred to in Somerset County as "big water." I remember paying $950 for those decoys. I was sure that I had not only "lost it" but that I would never be able to get that much for any pair of decoys that I owned. Time proved me wrong, and I am grateful for that. Over the years, I made many trips to Crisfield to visit Lem Ward; Steve had died in 1976 and, sadly, I never knew him. But through an introduction by John Tawes, an old family friend and lifelong Crisfielder, I met Lem and paid many pleasant visits to the shop and family home. It always bothered me that fame and a little fortune came to them so late in life. However, it never seemed to concern Lem the least bit.

In 1982, I had an opportunity to visit a unique island of the Lower Bay region. My friend Robert Lankford of Marion, Somerset County, who was then Supervisor of Assessments of that county, did me a great favor and made arrangements for a tour of Smith Island. A unique place, it is a location that I would urge anyone who calls himself a Marylander to visit. We met in Crisfield and traveled by the mail boat to the island. I can clearly recall the wonderful English accents of the islanders who traveled with us.

Yellow-shafted flicker from Crisfield, carved by a Tyler, a Sterling, or a Ward

Arriving on the island, we made a short walk to the parking lot, and there sat a county pickup truck, switch key under the floor mat waiting for our arrival. Bob started the truck, which had no muffler; salt air had taken care of that years before. We traveled every road and saw every sight—there were great crab-sloughing sheds right over the marsh, neat houses, churches, and tiny little post offices. The meanest, nastiest biting insects that I have ever encountered inhabit the island. As we drove the narrow roads with deep, water-filled ditches on either side, I recalled photographs in the newspaper from just a few years before of wheelbarrows filled with dead redhead ducks killed by a few Smith Island outlaws. I hoped that that practice was over for good. A reservation had been made for lunch at Mrs. Kitching's. We walked in, were greeted, sat down, and the biggest and lumpiest crab cakes in the world appeared before us. Two other travelers from our boat walked in and were quickly dismissed by Mrs. Kitching, "Sorry," she said "but I am entertaining special guests today." When the crab cakes were about three-quarters finished, she said, "I don't hear anything. Well, how are they?" "Excellent," I said, "The best I've ever had," and in an instant another platter appeared before us. I doubt that I will ever have that experience again. After lunch we were invited into the parlor, and introduced to Mr. Kitching. "I hear you like decoys, Bob tells me." "Yes sir," I replied. "Well then have a look at this Ward and tell me what you think of her." It was a hen pintail in original paint, and it was for sale to me. Well, I liked it something awful and it made the trip home with me, erasing the sting of those bug bites and making the entire memory as excellent as the crab cakes.

The Unknown Carver

*I*N THE MIDST of all of the excitement associated with one of the recent Easton Waterfowl Festivals, my son suggested to me that he had reached a conclusion as to who was the most important decoy maker of all time. He envisioned an entire display devoted to works by this famous artisan. He also felt that an appropriate article should be written, since no other text has ever been written concerning this decoy maker.

Every decoy text available, starting with *Wild Fowl Decoys* by Joel Barber, the first of this genre, mentions this carver. His work has been photographed more than any other decoy carver's work. Most decoy auctions include representative works by this maker. Record prices for his work have been established over and over with each successive auction. His earliest known works were discovered in 1924: eleven decoys formed from bulrushes were found in the Lovelock Indian Caves in Nevada. Collectors will remember that find as one of the most important to the overall history of the decoy. The University of Nevada used the carbon-14 method to date these decoys, which appear to hail from 100 B.C.

Aside from producing some of the most photographed and most admired work, this maker was also the most prolific. There is not a well-known collection that does not include some of his folk art nor has there ever been a major exhibit of Americana that did not include carvings by his hands. Every North American museum includes decoys by this maker among their collections. In the August 1932 edition of *Fortune* magazine, Joel Barber published for the first time a photograph of a fine example of the classic Chesapeake Bay canvasback of the 1880s by this maker; legend insists that President Grover Cleveland, one of the most sporting of all U.S. presidents, gunned over this decoy.

This decoy maker's carvings transcend time and region. His painting techniques are without a doubt some of the most realistic ever produced. His works will be remembered not as *some* of the most important but as the most important of all time. The next time you sit down with a book on historic decoys, or with an auction catalog from one of the major decoy auction houses, or visit a decoy exhibit, look for the work of this most important carver. A clue to his identity is best revealed by Joel Barber who so aptly put it in 1932: "the search for the decoy maker is the search for an honest artist." This artist's work will always be identified in the same way—"Maker Unknown."

There are many decoys whose creators will never be identified, but, from time to time, the identity of a previously unknown carver comes to light. In the fall of 2001, I was asked to identify and value a group of decoys for an upcoming auction in Havre de Grace. I visited the site with the auctioneer, Patrick S. O'Neill, as always in the hope of viewing some great trove of historic duck decoys and hoping that I would know the maker of whatever I saw. It is a self-imposed challenge of sorts, a test of my ability to remember what I've looked at before and to recall the maker's name and when he produced his work. What I came upon that day was a group of 750 duck and goose decoys, most of which had never left the owner's storehouse. He had used them himself and given some to family and friends over the years, but he had never sold one. The auctioneer and I were the first to handle the rig since they were retired to storage.

Among the decoys, I identified ones carved by Mitchell, Gibson, and Currier. But there were others that resembled the decoys of Madison Mitchell, Paul Gibson, James Currier, Harry Jobes, and James Holly, who have made decoys in Havre de Grace over the last 150 years. A group of black ducks had some of the best scratch painting that I had ever seen, and the carver had signed his name in the painting on the underside of them.

Black duck, Upper Chesapeake Bay, circa 1915

Ruddy duck drake, Upper Chesapeake Bay, circa 1870

Black duck carved by S. Lee Bowman of Havre de Grace, Maryland, unknown until October 2001

Underside of black duck showing signature of carver, S. Lee Bowman, Havre de Grace, Maryland

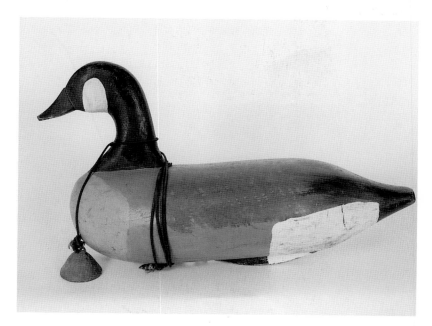

Canada goose by S. Lee Bowman, Havre de Grace, Maryland

The mallard decoys were in the best paint style used by Madison Mitchell on his very first mallard decoys. The few miniatures in the group did exactly what they are supposed to do, replicate the full-size decoys in every detail. This was a skilled carver and an excellent painter. The decoys were large, sturdy, outstanding working decoys in the Upper Bay style. All of the well-known carvers' artistic abilities had been combined in the work of one man's hands. My first inclination, therefore, was to identify the decoys as "committee birds," a term I have used to identify decoys that are the combined efforts of two or more carvers working on the same decoy. The carver, it turned out, was a lifelong resident of Havre de Grace who had worked with many of the carvers of that town. This 83-year-old carver advised that they were his work alone.

The auction was held, and each of the decoys brought a respectable price. The Mitchells, Gibsons, and Curriers were sold alongside the work of a *now known carver,* Sappington Lee Bowman, who sat and watched his lifetime's work being scattered among the many collectors in attendance. An unknown carver was identified the day of the sale; let Mr. Bowman be added to the list of known carvers.

Epilogue *Advice to a Collector*

I COLLECT THINGS, stuff, various and sundry items, which I, for some reason, consider important. In my particular case, the collecting started when I was quite young. My "collection" then consisted of a couple of pocket knives, a BB gun, some little plastic rings and things that came in cereal boxes, pieces of string, an occasional hubcap, the V-8 emblem from a 1950 Ford, and a few old wooden decoys. Most everyone I have known has collected something.

When my paternal grandfather died, he left me his pocket watch, pocketknives, one of his old shotguns (I had already found another), and mementos of forty-four years of employment with the Maryland and Pennsylvania Railroad. When my maternal grandfather died, I was presented with his grandfather's 1842 Colt pocket model, shotgun, rifle, and hand tools, and the wooden measuring bucket from his lifetime as a miller. Neither grandfather would have considered their stuff official "collections" but, rather, things that were either essential to their lives or things that were handed down to them. I am sure that I was so fond of these things as a young boy not because I was a collector but rather because they gave me a sense of my roots. But as I have found, stuff has a way of attracting more stuff. The half-dozen decoys that I had inherited by age thirteen certainly started something.

After acquiring wooden fowl with a passion for over thirty years, I suppose I am now considered an old-time decoy collector. This "seniority" in the decoy field leads new collectors to occasionally come to me for advice. Newer collectors seek out the seasoned collectors to ask whose decoys to collect. Many first-time collectors want to know which carver's work will be the best investment. My feelings, though usually suppressed, are to suggest to these collectors that they would perhaps be better off collecting stocks or bonds, because they are simply acquiring things for their investment potential and not because they appreciate the art of the decoy.

The true collector of decoys must initially appreciate the history of the decoy as America's unique contribution to the art world. Second, they must be able to see the beauty in nature in order to appreciate the beauty of the counterfeit wooden fowl. Finally, they must understand that these decoys were used as tools of the trade and their significance to the early hunter was like that of the hammer to the early carpenter, an important tool.

Part of a flock of about 5,000 Canada geese, at East Neck Island. Photograph by W. Bryant Tyrrell, December 13, 1937.

Beyond those basic criteria, my advice to a beginning collector is very simple; collect what you like, but do it within certain parameters or with some system. The following bases could be used for establishing a decoy collection:

A specific area, e.g., decoys from the various flyways, the Susquehanna Flats, Havre de Grace, the Chesapeake, or the Mid-Atlantic region

A specific maker or factory, e.g., Bob McGaw, Jim Currier, Paul Gibson, or the Ward brothers

A particular species, e.g., swan, Canada geese, canvasbacks, bluebills

Types of decoys, e.g., working bird, decorative model, or miniatures

Style of decoy, e.g., sleepers, preeners, high-heads, or swimmers

Following these basics, a collection may be built and refined over a period of time. I suggest that collectors look for such important features as original paint and original heads. Collectors must be aware that many fakes exist in the marketplace. I have seen some of the best experts fooled by high-quality "reproductions." The term *caveat emptor* must never escape the collector's mind. Legitimate dealers will advise a potential collector of all available information on a decoy. If that dealer will not, surely a competitor will. My personal experience in collecting and doing business with "decoy dealers" has been a very pleasant one. Seeking out the accoutrements to complement a collection will ultimately generate as much pleasure as acquiring the decoys themselves.

I would also like to give a word of advice to potential collectors about decoy maintenance. Decoys, whether old or new, are made of wood; and the wood will crack and split, or the decoy head will rise from its shelf. To minimize this, I suggest keeping decoys away from direct sunlight and intense heat. Areas in close proximity to a wood stove, fireplace, or heat vent should be avoided for collection display. Much has been written and discussed about surface finishes. A few collectors cannot leave well enough alone; they must make their mark on each piece they acquire. I have seen wonderful painted surfaces practically destroyed by collectors who insist on washing their latest acquisition with a scouring pad or harsh detergent. I watched a pair of decoys sell at Sotheby's in New York City in January of 2000 for a third less than they should have because a collector had scrubbed the birds and removed 100 years of patina. I recommend leaving time alone to enhance the beauty of a painted wooden decoy. Nothing beats a natural time-enhanced patina. Let time be the best friend to your collection. If anything is to be done to the surface, a light dusting once a month is my best recommendation.

My final word of advice to a new collector is to acquire that in which you find beauty. Never lose sight of the most important fact in collecting; we are only caretakers for a short time. We hope that, at the end of our caretaking, someone else will enjoy these things as much as we have.

To own a historic decoy is to own more than a block of wood. It is a piece of art and a time capsule of waterfowling history. We reflect on and appreciate where the decoy was made, for whom it was made, where it has been, and the great times to which it has contributed.

UPPER BAY

Algard, Carroll Cleveland "Wally." Charlestown, Cecil County, 1883–1959. Algard carved only canvasback decoys. His birds have the shelf carving and straight tail associated with the Cecil County style. An unusual hump rises on the back immediately in front of the paddle tail.

Barnard, Charles Nelson. Havre de Grace, Harford County, 1876–1958. Charles Nelson Barnard is best known for his high-neck canvasbacks. His decoys differ from those of other Havre de Grace carvers in having a paddle tail and a carved shelf for the neck to rest upon.

Barnard, Frederick T. Havre de Grace, Harford County, 1905–1991. Son of Charles Nelson Barnard, Fred made mostly canvasbacks and a few geese. His decoys were made for his own use. Many of his decoy bodies were turned on the lathe in Madison Mitchell's shop.

Barnard, Thomas P. Havre de Grace, Harford County, 1874–1927. Thomas Barnard made only canvasbacks. Like his brother Charles, he is best known for his bold high-neck. Some of his decoys were made without a distinct shelf, and his paddle tails are more subtle than those of Charles's decoys. Few examples are known.

Barnes, George Washington. Carpenter's Point, Cecil County, 1861–1915. Barnes operated a fishing camp with his brothers at the mouth of the North East River. He carved only canvasbacks and black ducks in the Cecil County style.

Barnes, Samuel Treadway. Havre de Grace, Harford County, 1857–1926. Barnes was the first carver in the region to exhibit in a decoy show, winning first prize for his canvasback decoys in New York City in 1924. He was also the first decoy carver from Havre de Grace to produce decoys using cork. Barnes's sons Herbert and Sam also carved some full-size decoys and some miniatures.

Bowman, Sappington Lee. Havre de Grace, Harford County, 1918–2002. Bowman, who was born near Rock Run, close to the Susquehanna River, lived in Harford County throughout his lifetime and was employed as a carpenter at the Aberdeen Proving Ground. He carved Canada geese, mallards, and black ducks from 1948 to 1960, but his production consisted of no more than a few hundred decoys. They were made for his own use and not for sale. His scratch-painted black ducks are among the best from the region.

Boyd, Taylor L. Perryville, Cecil County, 1856–1946. Boyd carved canvasbacks, redheads, bluebills, and black ducks. Each exhibits a very distinct paddle tail and carved mandibles. One ever-present characteristic is a notch carved where the tail joins the body.

Cockey, James. Stevensville, Kent Island, Queen Anne's County, 1893–1971. Cockey carved swans, Canada geese, canvasbacks, bluebills, and redheads. He built boats for use on the Chesapeake, and his skill as a boat builder is reflected in his well-designed decoys. One of his magnificent swan decoys is in the collection of the Maryland Historical Society.

Coudon, Joseph. Aiken, Cecil County, 1860–1947. Coudon is best known for his silhouette V-boards—floating, folding racks of duck cutouts. There were three cutouts per board, and they were sold in wooden boxes, four sets to the box. Coudon received a U.S. patent for this "Device for Decoying Ducks" on June 25, 1901. Most species of ducks were represented among his silhouettes. Coudon was an accomplished artist, and several of his bas-relief dioramas with wildfowl exist in well-known collections. Joel Barber pictured Coudon's carvings of the now-extinct passenger pigeon in *Wild Fowl Decoys*.

Currier, James A. Havre de Grace, Harford County, 1886–1971. Currier was the postmaster of Havre de Grace for many years. Each of his decoys was hand chopped, and those remaining in original paint show a light feathering on their backs and speculums. His production was primarily canvasbacks, redheads, bluebills, and Canada geese, although later in life he carved all species. His miniature decoys were unusual in that the body and head sizes varied, which apparently resulted from his use of whatever size wood was available.

Davis, Henry. Perryville, Cecil County, 1875–1956. Davis carved canvasbacks with his fishing partner, Asa Owens. His decoys exhibit a pronounced V-bottom, with a flat surface in their centers and a wider, blunt tail than most decoys from the Upper Bay.

Dye, Benjamin. Perryville, Cecil County, 1821–1896. Benjamin Dye's decoys demonstrate some of the finest carving and detail work of the early Susquehanna Flats carvers. He lived at Stump's Point on the Susquehanna Flats, making decoys for his own use, gunning clubs, and guides for the region. He carved canvasbacks, redheads, bluebills, and black ducks. A few diminutive ruddy ducks have been attributed to him.

Dye, Joseph E. Havre de Grace, Harford County, 1870–1931. A son of Benjamin Dye who moved to Havre de Grace in 1890, Joseph Dye carved his decoys in the Cecil County style, with a raised shelf and elongated paddle tail. He painted very few of his decoys as hens. He is best known for his original-paint bluebills, which show strong wing patterns on their backs.

Fletcher, Columbus Paxton. Havre de Grace, Harford County, 1867–1942. Fletcher is known to have carved only canvasbacks, most with a higher than average head. Each of his decoys exhibits a rather blunt upswept tail.

Gibson, Paul. Havre de Grace, Harford County, 1902–1985. Gibson worked as a fireman on the Aberdeen Proving Ground. His earliest decoys were hand chopped. In the late 1930s, his production changed and he turned bodies on a duplicating lathe. The style of his goldeneyes and teal was unique in the region. Many of his smaller carvings have a flat surface on the bottom for attaching a ballast weight. He carved most species, including full-sized swans and Canada geese. Some of his best-known carvings are preeners. His very first decoy was a miniature, which he carved in Samuel T. Barnes's decoy shop. He continued to produce a limited number of miniatures up until the 1950s. Like McGaw and Mitchell, he mounted his miniatures on walnut bases.

Graham, John Black. Charlestown, Cecil County, 1822–1912. Graham was a cabinetmaker and undertaker. His family probably produced thousands of decoys. Although his style changed through the years, all of his decoys exhibit a distinct shelf carving and bodies that are rounder than those of other decoys from the Flats. Several examples branded "J. B. Graham" have surfaced. He produced some of the earliest teal decoys from the region.

Heverin, William Y. Charlestown, Cecil County, 1863–1951. Like many carvers from the area, Heverin spent his lifetime hunting and fishing. Each of his decoys exhibits a strong shelf and an elongated paddle tail. Where the decoy's bill joins the head of the duck, a hint of a smile is evident. Heverin carved his decoys in a variety of sizes, depending upon what size wood was most available. He carved canvasbacks, redheads, bluebills, and black ducks.

Holly, James T. Havre de Grace, Harford County, 1855–1935. Holly was the last son born of John Holly, the most prolific of the early Havre de Grace carvers. James carved decoys and built bushwhack boats and sinkboxes throughout his lifetime. His black ducks, mallards, and pintails were among the sleekest and raciest birds carved in the town. He was one of the first to use the technique of scratch painting on some of his decoys. He carved swans, Canada geese, canvasbacks, redheads, bluebills, black ducks, pintails, mallards, and teal.

Holly, John "Daddy." Havre de Grace, Harford County, 1818–1892. Holly was the first known carver of what was to become the Havre de Grace style of decoys. A market hunter and fisherman as well as decoy carver, he is recognized in the earliest sporting histories of Havre de Grace as a skilled duck shooter. His two sons, John, Jr., (1852–1927) and William (1845–1923), lived next door to their father, and speculation has it that they helped with his decoy production. Many Holly decoys appear wearing the brands of gunners and gunning clubs from Long Island to North Carolina.

Jackson, W. Scott. Charlestown, Cecil County, 1852–1929. Jackson was a brother-in-law of decoy carver G. W. Barnes and a neighbor of William Heverin. Jackson decoys exhibit a slight upsweep to the tail. Most of his decoys show strong spoke shave markings. He is best known for his classic teal decoys. He also carved canvasbacks and redheads and is credited with making miniature decoys.

Litzenberg, Robert G., 1910–1966, and William, 1907–1975. Elkton, Cecil County. The Litzenberg brothers were painting contractors and made canvasback decoys for their own use. Their decoys were hand chopped, with paddle tails and heads similar to those carved by William Heverin.

Lockard, George, 1866–1931, and Henry, 1868–1944. Elk Neck, Cecil County. The Lockards carved decoys primarily for their own use. The carved nostrils of their decoys appear as half-moons in the bill. The paddle tails are shorter than those of most Cecil County carvers and show a slight upsweep. The Lockards carved only redheads and canvasbacks. They apparently never painted any of their own decoys. All of those found in original paint were painted by either Robert F. McGaw or John Glen.

McGaw, Robert F. Havre de Grace, Harford County, 1879–1958. McGaw was the first decoy carver in the region to use a duplicating lathe to turn out his bodies. The lathe process eliminated the need to hand chop a decoy body, but extensive use of hand tools was still required to shape them. They were in no way machine produced. His decoys appear in Joel Barber's book *Wild Fowl Decoys,* published in 1934. He made thousands of miniature decoys mounted on wooden bases and was among the first Havre de Grace carvers to produce full-size decorative decoys. He conducted a large mail-order business from his home, which has resulted in his decoys being widely distributed throughout the country. Each of his working decoys wears a dog-bone-shaped sheet lead ballast weight attached with five nails.

Mitchell, R. Madison. Havre de Grace, Harford County, 1901–1993. Undoubtedly the best-known Havre de Grace carver, Mitchell produced decoys from 1924 through the 1980s. He was a full-time funeral director in the city of Havre de Grace throughout his lifetime. His carving spans the time of the sinkbox and market hunters to the decorative decoys of today. He carved all species of waterfowl known to the Upper Chesapeake region. Many decorative carvings that Mitchell referred to as "Christmas ducks" are known in collections. He carved miniature decoys from the 1940s until the early 1960s. From 1929, his decoys were all lathe-turned and exhibited the Havre de Grace style. His pattern was based on the style of John "Daddy" Holly. Mitchell is credited with instructing dozens of young men in the art of decoy carving, and his former students continue to produce decoys in the Mitchell style and tradition.

Moltz, Bailey. Havre de Grace, Harford County, 1888–1963. His whole life, Moltz lived on the waterfront in Havre de Grace. He carved heads for various decoy makers in town as well as many full-sized working decoys, mostly canvasbacks, mallard, and Canada geese, for sale and for his own use. His decoy heads are often described as "boardheads" because of their flat sides.

Pearson, Edwin E. Havre de Grace, Harford County, 1859–1932. Pearson owned a lumberyard in Havre de Grace and produced bushwhack boats for sale. He is listed as an hourly employee in James Holly's ledger. He made canvasback decoys, many of which are branded "E. Pearson." All of his decoys have larger than average heads.

Pryor, Leonard E. Chesapeake City, Cecil County, 1876–1967. Some of Pryor's work was produced in the typical Cecil County style, while other of his decoys more closely resemble the work of Delaware River carvers. His decoy tails are always slightly upswept, and the nostrils appear similar in style to the decoys of the Lockard brothers. Several canvasbacks carved as sleepers or preeners have been discovered. Besides canvasbacks, he made bluebills, black ducks, and pintails. His black ducks and pintails were hollow-carved.

Simpers, Dick. Havre de Grace, Harford County. Simpers was a guide for Captain Harry Moore, who owned the gunning scow the *Jennie Moore.* He is known to have carved only canvasbacks. He carved in the Havre de Grace style, his decoys showing a slightly upswept tail. His heads were well carved, with details including nostrils.

Thomas, Al. Swan Creek, Aberdeen, Harford County, 1873–1953. Thomas carved only canvasbacks. They were large sturdy decoys with heavy bills, often referred to as "shoebills," because the underside of the bill was shaped something like the sole of a shoe.

Watson, J. Milton. Chesapeake City, Cecil County, 1911–1985. Watson carved in the Cecil County tradition. His high-neck canvasbacks are his best-known work. He made bushwhack boats and became one of the first carvers in the region to produce miniature bushwhack boats and rigs of miniature decoys.

Webb, Clarence, Jr. Elkton, Cecil County, 1907–1994. Webb gunned with live geese until the practice was outlawed in 1935. His wooden decoys, made in the style of Havre de Grace carvers, were for his own use only. He carved canvasbacks, bluebills, pintails, and coot. He also made one rig of Canada geese, of cork with one-inch pine bottom boards.

MIDDLE BAY

Creighton, Clarence Hix "Pap." Hooper's Island, Dorchester County, 1885–?. Creighton carved decoys for use with his own rig and for others in the vicinity of Hooper's Island. He made canvasbacks, bluebills, and goldeneyes. He is most famous for his "folky" mergansers and diminutive buffleheads. He employed various materials for ballast weights on his decoys, including chain, horseshoes, and scrap iron.

Elliott, William, 1907–1983, and Chank, 1907–1975. Easton, Talbot County. Identical twins, William and Chank Elliott were house painters by trade. Their decoys were more crudely finished than most but lightweight and sturdy. They are best known for their cork-bodied root-headed swans and geese.

Glen, John. Rock Hall, Kent County, 1876–1954. Glen carved Canada geese and most species of ducks. None of his decoys are finish sanded, and therefore spoke shave marks are evident. The very first goose silhouettes for field shooting are attributed to Glen.

Heinefield, August George. Rock Hall, Kent County, 1883–1952. Born in Germany, Heinefield moved to Kent County as a child; he was engaged in the carpentry trade and worked for John Glen making decoys. He produced only several hundred decoys on his own. His decoys exhibit a strong upswept tail, and most species are represented in his body of work.

Meekins, "Gunner" Alvin. Hooper's Island, Dorchester County. Meekins is most famous for his red-breasted mergansers and buffleheads. He made flying decoys with wire-formed canvas-covered wings.

Parsons, Edward T. Oxford, Talbot County, 1856–1937. With the exception of the Elliott brothers, Parsons was the only commercial decoy maker in Talbot County. His decoys are smaller than most, yet well rounded. He turned to miniature carving in 1931. His father, Thomas Parsons, was also a decoy carver in Talbot County. Edward concentrated on diving ducks, including buffleheads, goldeneyes, and bluebills. Later on he added canvasbacks and redheads. He is credited with using a recessed circular lead weight in the bottom of his decoys, a practice later copied by many other carvers from Talbot County.

Phillips, Edward James. Cambridge, Dorchester County, 1901–1964. Phillips was not a commercial decoy maker but made birds for his own use. He carved rounded, refined decoys, taking great pains with intricate paint patterns. His pintails, widgeons, and Canada geese exhibit the best of his work. He also produced canvasbacks, redheads, and bluebills. His bluebills are the only examples of his carvings which were hollowed out. He made a number of miniature decoys.

Travers, Josiah F. Vienna, Dorchester County, 1900–1965. Travers was one of the few Middle Bay carvers to make use of cork. His decoys had pine heads and bottom boards. Some examples are known to have the heads attached with screen door springs to hold them in place; the spring also gave the heads motion in rough waters. Some of his wooden decoys exhibit a curious humpback or turtleback appearance. The finest examples of Travers' decoys are his widgeons, but he also carved Canada geese and black ducks.

Urie, Jesse. Rock Hall, Kent County, 1901–1978. Urie hand chopped his decoys at his shop next to John Glen's. His decoy operation developed from assisting Glen in his production. Urie began turning his bodies on a lathe in 1955. By 1968, his production changed from working decoys to miniature decoys, which were identical in style to his full-size gunning decoys. There is a flat area evident on the breast of each bird, which resulted from trimming the lathe-turned body.

Vickers, John. Cambridge, Dorchester County. Vickers made only black ducks and swans.

Lower Bay

Sterling, Lloyd. Crisfield, Somerset County, 1880–1964. Lloyd Sterling carved flat-bottomed decoys in the Crisfield style. His humpback pintails and widgeons are his best-known work. A relationship apparently existed between Sterling and the Ward brothers, since some of the Sterling decoys appear in original Ward brothers paint.

Sterling, Noah Bernard. Crisfield, Somerset County, 1885–1954. Noah Sterling, a boat builder by trade, carved decoys that are somewhat crude but sturdy. Most are oversized and are characterized by high, round backs and rather narrow breasts that slope down to the flat bottoms.

Tyler, Lloyd J. Crisfield, Somerset County, 1898–1970. Tyler lived directly across the road from the Ward brothers for most of his life. There is a naïveté evident in each of his carvings, and few are as finely finished as carvings by the Wards and Sterlings. Each of his decoys has a flat bottom. He never painted the undersides of his decoys, oft-times saying "painting bottoms is a waste of paint and time." Tyler referred to himself as the poor man's decoy maker.

Walker, Robert C. Ocean City, Worcester County, 1894–1971. Walker carved shore birds from pine and cedar and made flatties (silhouettes) from sheet tin, as did his father, William, before him. He fashioned his wildfowl decoys from cork, creating bluebills, redheads, canvasbacks, black ducks, and Canada geese. His geese had root heads in alert positions. The necks had a dowel rod in their bottom which exited through a copper-lined hole in the breast. Into the bottom of the dowel was inserted a screw eye, to which the decoy's anchor line was attached. He made decoys for his own use and for his sons'.

Ward, Lemuel T., 1896–1984, and Steven W., 1894–1979. Crisfield, Somerset County. The work of these two brothers is the best known of any carvers from the Chesapeake region. The Ward brothers began carving in their father's decoy shop as young men and produced some of the most beautiful carvings of the Bay. Steve did most of the carving, while brother Lem's painting skills excelled. Throughout their years of production, they created decoys in many styles of each species. The Ward Foundation opened the Ward Museum of Wildfowl Art in 1971 as a dedication to the brothers.

Ward, L. Travis. Crisfield, Somerset County, 1873–1926. L. Travis Ward, father of Lemuel and Steven, was the first recognized carver of the Lower Bay. Since most of his decoys were used on the shallow marshes throughout the county, they featured wide, flat bottoms, unlike the decoys used farther up the Bay. Many of his decoys are oversized. Ward also built boats and ran a barbershop throughout his lifetime. His sons began working around the decoy shop at an early age.

☼ SOURCES ☼

"Add Americana: The Decoy." *Fortune* (August 1932): 38–42.

"An All-American Dog." *Forest and Stream* (September 1916): 727–28.

The American Shooter's Manual, Comprising Such Plain and Simple Rules as Are Necessary To Introduce the Inexperienced into a Full Knowledge of All That Relates to the Dog, and the Correct Use of the Gun; also a Description of the Game of this Country by a Gentleman of Philadelphia County. 1827. Reprint, New York: Ernest R. Gee, 1928.

Baltimore City Business Directory for 1858–1859. Baltimore, Md.: J.C. & H.Q. Nicholson, 1859.

Barber, Joel. *Wild Fowl Decoys.* New York: Winward House, 1934.

Bishops Head Fish and Gun Club. *Journal of the Bishops Head Fish and Gun Club,* November 2, 1925–January 30, 1926. From the collection of Grayson Winterbottom III.

Bliss, Anthony A., ed. *The Chesapeake Bay Retriever,* revised ed. New York: American Chesapeake Club, 1936.

Blogg, Percy Thayer. *There Are No Dull Dark Days.* Baltimore: H. G. Roebuck & Son, 1944.

———. Photo album, August 1911. From the collection of C. John Sullivan.

Brugger, Robert J. *Maryland: A Middle Temperament, 1634–1980.* Baltimore: Johns Hopkins University Press, 1988.

Burges, Arnold. *The American Kennel and Sporting Field.* Brooklyn, N.Y.: D.S. Holmes, 1882.

Cadwalader, John. Asset books, 1845–1917. From the collection of C. John Sullivan.

Carroll's Island Ducking Club. Minutes 1851–65. Baltimore County Public Library, Towson, Md.

———. Record of Game Killed. MS 2807, Manuscripts Division, Maryland Historical Society, Baltimore, Md.

"Carroll's Island Duck-Shooting." *Forest and Stream* (April 13, 1882): 208.

Cecil County Agricultural Society. Pamphlet for the Fifth Annual Fair of the Cecil County Agricultural Society on October 7–10, 1884. From the collection of C. John Sullivan.

"Chesapeake Dog as a Retriever." *The Sportsmen's Review* (April 1, 1916).

"Chesapeake's Origin." *Hunting and Fishing* (November 1933): 31.

Clark & Sneider. "The Sneider Patent Double-Barrel, Breech-Loading Shot Gun, Double and Single Solid Grip Top Lever, using either Paper or Metal

Shells, Manufactured only by Clark & Sneider, 214 W. Pratt Street, Baltimore, Md. Printed at the Office of the 'Maryland Farmer,' No. 141 West Pratt Street. 1878." MS 1262, Manuscripts Division, Maryland Historical Society Library, Baltimore, Md.

Cleveland, Grover. *Fishing and Shooting Sketches.* New York: Outing Publishing, 1906.

Cooke, May Thacher. "Birds of the Washington, D.C., Region." Proceedings of the Biological Society of Washington, March 25, 1929.

Coues, Elliott, and D. Webster Prentiss. *Avifauna Columbiana: Being a List of Birds Ascertained To Inhabit the District of Columbia, with the Times of Arrival and Departure of Such as Are Non-Resident, and Brief Notices of Habits, etc.,* 2nd ed. Washington, D.C.: Government Printing Office, 1883.

Cypress, J., Jr. *Sporting Scenes and Sundry Sketches.* Vols. 1 and 2. Frank Forester, ed. New York: Gould, Banks, 1842.

Department of the Interior. *Bulletin of the United States National Museum,* no. 26. Washington: Government Printing Office, 1883.

"Duck Shooting." *American Agriculturalist* 27 (1868): 361.

Dyke, Samuel H. "The Crisfield Carvers." *Ward Foundation News* (Summer 1981): 8–11.

———. "What's in a Name? The Oft-misidentified Decoys of Noah Bernard Sterling." *Decoy Magazine* (May–June 1994): 8–11.

Eildon Ducking Club. *Journal of the Eildon Ducking Club,* 1886–97. Copyright Anthony Hillman, Cape May Court House, N.J.

Engers, Joe. "Chesapeake Bay Gunning Decoys." *Maryland* (Autumn 1991): 14–23.

Fleckenstein, Henry A., Jr. *Decoys of the Mid-Atlantic Region.* Exton, Pa.: Schiffer Publishing, 1979.

Forester, Frank, ed. *The Dog by Dinks, Mayhew, and Hutchinson.* New York: Stringer & Townsend, 1857.

Game Division, Conservation Department of Maryland. *Conservation Laws of Maryland Relating to Wild Fowl, Birds, Game and Fish.* Effective June 1, 1924 to June 1, 1927. Game Division of Maryland, Baltimore, Md.

Giraud, J. P., Jr. *The Birds of Long Island.* New York: Wiley & Putnam, 1844.

Goodwin, Butch. *The Chesapeake Bay Retriever.* New Plymouth, Idaho: Northern Flight Retrievers, 1999. Photocopy.

Graham, Joseph A. *The Sporting Dog.* New York: Macmillan, 1904.

Grinnell, George Bird. *American Duck Shooting.* New York: Forest and Stream Publishing, 1901.

Gunther, Roy. "Charles Edward Sneider, Gunsmith/Inventor." *The Gun Report* 37, no. 12 (May 1992): 16–28.

Harewood, Harry. *A Dictionary of Sports; or, Companion to the Field, the Forest, and the Riverside.* London: Tegg & Son, 1835.

Harford County Assessment Office. Assessor's Books for 1st, 2nd, and 6th Districts, 1896. Harford Co., Md.

———. Assessor's Book, 1896. City of Havre de Grace, Md.

———. Tax Assessors Schedules and Returns of Real and Personal Property, 1896–1902. Harford Co., Md.

Hazelton, William C. "The Chesapeake Bay Dog." *Maryland Conservationist* (Fall 1928): 7–11.

Hazelton, William C., ed. *Tales of Duck and Goose Shooting.* Springfield, Illinois: Press of Phillips Bros., 1922.

Herbert, Henry William. *American Game in Its Seasons.* New York: Charles Scribner, 1853.

———. *Frank Forester's Field Sports of the United States and British Provinces of North America.* Vols. 1 and 2. New York: W. A. Townsend, 1866.

Hercules Powder Company. *Field and Trap Shooting.* Wilmington, Del.: Hercules Powder Company, 1923.

"Historic and Modern Decoys." *The Sportsman* (September 1934): 27.

Holly, James T. Ledger, 1886–1917. Private collection.

Hornaday, William T. *The Statement of the Permanent Wild Life Protection Fund, 1913–1914.* New York: Permanent Wild Life Protection Fund, March 1915.

Judd, Sylvester D. *Birds of a Maryland Farm, a Local Study of Economic Ornithology.* Washington, D.C.: U.S. Department of Agriculture, 1902.

Kirkwood, F. C. *A List of the Birds of Maryland.* Baltimore: Maryland Academy of Sciences, 1895.

Klapp, H. Milnor, ed. *Krider's Sporting Anecdotes, Illustrative of the Habits of Certain Varieties of American Game.* Philadelphia: A. Hart, 1853.

Latrobe, Ferdinand C. "A Generation Ago." *Maryland Conservationist* (Summer 1936): 8–9.

———. *Iron Men and Their Dogs.* Baltimore: Ivan R. Drechsler, 1941.

Letter of John Cadwalader to Charles Raymond, May 20, 1891: From the collection of C. John Sullivan.

Letter of John D. Smith to Robert F. McGaw, September 1860: From the collection of C. John Sullivan.

Lewis, Elisha J. *The American Sportsman: containing Hints to Sportsmen, Notes on Shooting, and the Habits of the Game Birds and Wild Fowl of America.* Philadelphia: J. B. Lippincott, 1857.

Lloyd, Freeman. "Kennel, Bench and Field." *The Sportsman* (June 1932): 65–66.

Long, Joseph W. *American Wild-Fowl Shooting. Describing the Haunts, Habits, and Method of Shooting Wild-Fowl, Particularly Those of the Western States of America.* New York: J. B. Ford, 1874.

Mackey, William J., Jr. *American Bird Decoys.* New York: E. P. Dutton, 1965.

Manning, Thomas. *The American Yacht List for 1892.* New York: Thomas Manning, 1892.

Marksman. *The Dead Shot; or, Sportsman's Complete Guide: Being a Treatise on the Use of the Gun, with Rudimentary and Finishing Lessons in the Art of Shooting Game of All Kinds: Pigeon-Shooting, Dog-Breaking, etc.* New York: W. A. Townsend, 1864.

Marshy Point Ducking Club. Journal of the Marshy Point Ducking Club, Baltimore Co., Md., 1854–84. From the collection of Harry C. Weiskittel III.

———. Marshy Point Guest Book, May 26, 1923–November 27, 1970. From the collection of Harry C. Weiskittel III.

Maryland Historical Society. *Chesapeake Wildfowl Hunting: Maryland's Finest Decoys. Maryland Historical Society Exhibit September 27, 1991–February 2, 1992.* Baltimore: Museum and Library of Maryland History, Maryland Historical Society, 1991.

Maxwell's Point Visitors' Book, Harford Co., Md., 1887–1917. From the collection of C. John Sullivan.

Mayer, Alfred M., ed. *Sport with Gun and Rod.* New York: Century, 1883.

McCullough, David. *John Adams.* New York: Simon & Schuster, 2001.

McKinney, J. Evans. *Decoys of the Susquehanna Flats and Their Makers.* Ocean City, Md.: Decoy Magazine, 1978.

Phillips, John C., and Lewis Webb Hill, eds. *Classics of the American Shooting Field: A Mixed Bag for the Kindly Sportsman, 1783–1926.* Boston: Houghton Mifflin, 1930.

Portrait and Biographical Record of Harford and Cecil Counties Maryland. New York: Chapman Publishing, 1897.

Pough, Richard H. *Audubon Water Bird Guide. Water, Game and Large Land Birds. Eastern and Central North America from Southern Texas to Central Greenland.* Sponsored by National Audubon Society. Garden City, N.Y.: Doubleday, 1951.

Pusey, Joel. Ledger, 1916–36. From the collection of C. John Sullivan.

———. Gunning account, November 2, 1925–November 17, 1926. From the collection of C. John Sullivan.

Pusey, Joel, and Clarence C. Pusey. Ledgers, 1878–1918. From the collection of C. John Sullivan.

Pusey, John. Hunting and trapping book, 1929–30. From the collection of C. John Sullivan.

———. Gunning account, April 8, 1931–May 1932. From the collection of C. John Sullivan.

Rough Ashlar. Journal. From the collection of the Maryland Historical Society Library, Baltimore, Md.

Samuels, Edward A. *Ornithology and Oology of New England.* Boston: Nichols & Noyes, 1867.

Seneca River Ducking Club. Seneca River Ducking Club logs, 1855–68. MS 734, Manuscripts Division, Maryland Historical Society Library, Baltimore, Md.

Skinner, J. S. *The Dog and the Sportsman.* Philadelphia: Lea & Blanchard, 1845.

Smith, Harry Worcester. *A Sporting Family of the Old South.* Albany, N.Y.: J. B. Lyon Company, 1936.

The Sportsman's Portfolio of American Field Sports. 1855. Reprint, New York: Ernest R. Gee, Derrydale Press, 1929.

Spraker, Capt. Harry W. *The Story of Gunpowder Neck.* Edgewood Arsenal, Maryland, 1926. Privately published pamphlet.

Stansbury, Henry H. *Lloyd Tyler: Folk Artist Decoy Maker.* Burtonsville, Md.: Decoy Magazine, 1995.

Stewart, Gail, ed. *The Cabinet of Natural History and American Rural Sports with Illustrations.* 1830, 1832, and 1833. Reprint, Barre, Mass.: Imprint Society, 1973.

Sullivan, C. John, Jr. *Waterfowling: The Upper Chesapeake's Legacy.* Fallston, Md.: Maplehurst Publishers, 1987.

———. "The Dignified Upper Chesapeake Bay Decoys of Charles Nelson Barnard." *Decoy Magazine* (November–December 1989): 16–19.

———. "The Unknown Carver." *Decoy Magazine* (November–December 1990): 24–25.

———. "A Cameo on Conservation." *Decoy Magazine* (May–June 1991): 24–26.

———. "The Hollys of Havre de Grace." *Decoy Magazine* (January–February 1992): 8–13.

———. "Paul Gibson: Decoy Maker and Painter." *The Canvasback* (Fall 1992): 16–21.

———. "The Deadliest Device." *The Canvasback* (Winter 1993): 16–18.

———. "Samuel Treadway Barnes." *Decoy Magazine* (March–April 1993): 8–11.

———. "Robert F. McGaw, Jr." *The Canvasback* (Spring 1994): 28–34.

———. "A Whiteness of Swan." *The Canvasback* (Fall 1994): 12–14.

———. "Historic Branded Decoys of the Susquehanna Flats." *Decoy Magazine* (March–April 1995): 14–15.

———. "The Era of the Sinkbox." *Decoy Magazine* (November–December 1995): 24–27.

———. "The Grahams of Charlestown." *Decoy Magazine* (July–August 1997): 8–13.

———. "The Hollys of Havre de Grace." *Wildfowl Art* (journal of the Ward Museum) (Spring–Summer 1998): 22–23.

———. "Ducking Clubs of the Upper Chesapeake Bay." *The Canvasback* (Fall 1998): 8–26.

———. "Waterfowling on the Upper Chesapeake." *Maryland Humanities* (March 1999): 2–5.

———. "Charles Nelson Barnard." *The Canvasback* (Spring 2001): 19–24.

———. "Teal Decoys of the Susquehanna Flats." *Decoy Magazine* (September–October 2001): 8–11.

Trumbull, Gurdon. *Names and Portraits of Birds Which Interest Gunners.* New York: Harper & Brothers, 1888.

Walker, Robert Craighead. Journal, 1904–16. From the collection of C. John Sullivan.

❊ Index ❊